Goblin

Dell

The Gothic Narratives of

David Lewis Paget

For my wife
and life companion
Lyn

Narrative Poetry by the same author:

Timepieces – Poems Out of Time & Other Places
At Journey's End – Narrative Poems Vol. II
The Demon Horse on the Carousel – and Other Gothic Delights
Poems of Myth & Scare
The Devil on the Tree – and Other Poems of Dysfunction
Tales from the Magi
Taking Root
The Storm and the Tall-Ship Pier
The Book on the Topmost Shelf
Tall Tales for Tired Times
Butterflies
The Widow of Martin Black

Lulu Spotlight at http://www.lulu.com/spotlight/david_lewis_paget

ISBN – 978-0-9596876-5-1

BARR BOOKS

Introduction

Welcome to Goblin Dell, the repository for yet another collection of narrative poems from my pen, the thirteenth. Within this colourful Dell are the imaginative streams of an alternative world, a world that we all visualise at times if only to escape the one we're in. This new world of ours doesn't adhere to the physical laws, rules and regulations that presently bind us. It transcends all that, being beholden only to the limits of our imaginations, taking us to distant countries and landscapes where we may meet the strange and untrammelled denizens of these regions without suffering their infections, or paying the price for their incapacities. Though they will fill your eyes and mind with the temporary shock of amazement, you will still be able to part from them, and find your way home, this I promise you.

But all the while, you will find a rhythm pounding in your head, that of a rhyme and metre that drives each story on through magical uplands, into dark, subterranean regions, and even the coastal areas that these tales inhabit. You may recognise in these stories people you know, traits you are familiar with, a karma that has revisited those unfortunate enough to have triggered it.

However, a word of warning. Lend this book out at your peril... you may never get it back!

David Lewis Paget   January 2016

Contents

Goblin Dell

He spoke of the stream that flowed uphill
In a grotto, long forgot,
Then said the stream would be flowing still,
And I could believe, or not.
I thought he was strange, with a twisted mind
For the concept was insane,
He said that he came from another time
In a land of eternal rain.

I'd met him at Janet's party where
He drifted from room to room,
Where everyone else was hearty but
He gave off an air of gloom.
I noticed one of his eyes was blue
The other was green, I'd say,
Whenever he stared they both were red
And his face became slate grey.

I'll never know why he spoke to me
I hadn't met him before,
He had this prominent artery
That ran the length of his jaw,
His voice was flat and unmusical
Though it said the strangest things,
The bones of knuckles were beautiful
He said, when covered in rings.

I followed him to the verandah where
I found him gazing at stars,
He said they seemed to be back to front
I said, 'Well at least, they're ours.'
'The grass I knew was a deeper blue,'
He said, 'and the sky was green,'
I said, 'You must be from out of town,
We would think that was obscene.'

He said 'You're not very friendly,' when
I thought we were doing fine,
He asked me to show him the number six
But I showed him the number nine.
That bus would take him to Goblin Dell
By the longest way around,
I said to myself, it's just as well
He'll end in the Lost and Found.

I still regret that I didn't go
To the grotto, long forgot,
He said he was willing to take me there
Whether I would, or not,
I'd like to have seen the fabled stream
That he said had flowed uphill,
And where it led to the source of dream
Where the rain is raining still.

A Chaste Affair

When the King rode off to the old Crusades
He was leaving his Queen behind,
Safe in the hands of his former aids
He was coy, but he wasn't blind.
He kept her locked in a chastity belt
And hid the key in his gaol,
Then swore the Gaoler to guard it well
Though the gaoler went quite pale.

How could he give a 'No' to a Queen,
Or 'No' to her favourite Earl,
So he perspired when the King retired
And travelled half round the world.
The Queen was troubled, she said it chafed
And demanded he give her the key,
'But no, My Lady, I wouldn't dare,
It would mean the end for me.'

'Do you think he'll even remember your face
By the time that he gets back home?
I'll have you gutted, and then replaced
While he's still out there to roam.
I'll ask the headsman to bring his axe,
The hangman to bring his rope,
And six fine horses to tear you apart
If you think there's a spark of hope.'

'Your pardon, Lady, I gave my oath
And am bound by the King's decree,
He swore I'd burn in a barrel of tar
If ever I give up the key.'
'Then I shall boil you in oil,' she said,
'And strip the skin from your bones,
I'll feed your fat to the pigs,' she said,
'And take delight in your moans.'

He sought protection from higher up,
The Earl had noticed his plight,
And said, 'I'll send you my personal guard
If you lend me the key one night.
I'll guard it well, and you'll get it back
When the sun comes up at dawn,
Not a word of this shall pass my lips
As I stand, an Earl has sworn.'

The gaoler gibbered in fear and grief
He could see his head on a spike,
'I can't conspire with your lord's desire
No matter how much I'd like.
The key is hid in a secret place
That is only known to the King,
He hid it where there would be no trace,
It's only a tiny thing.'

The Earl then sent his guards to the gaol
And they tore the place apart,
While searching for the chastity key
To settle his troubled heart.
The Queen sat in her apartments, on
A cushion of fine brocade,
It helped to ease where the belt had teased,
And hid where the Earl had played.

The key they found, hid under a slab
At the base of the dungeon door,
And soon the lovers were lain together
The chastity belt on the floor.
The months went by in a lovers sigh
Til the King and his knights rode back,
Their shields and helmets worn and dented
In Saladin's fierce attack.

The Queen's trim figure was rather large
When the key was put to the belt,
It's hard to know what a King would show,
And harder to know what he felt.
But he burnt the Earl in a barrel of tar
And the gaoler did what he said,
He lowered the Queen in a barrel of oil
Til it bubbled up over her head.

The Man that She Helped to Die

The Lord High Constable's men came down
To Camberwell's village square,
They asked the Crier to call Oyez
To gather the villagers there,
He rang his bell and the people came
Agog, when they heard him say,
A rogue they sought was abroad, they thought,
Was last seen heading their way.

'Beware this man, he's an evil rogue,
He battered his wife to death,
The woman lay in a blind dismay
Breathing her final breath,
If anyone sees a stranger here
Who looks like a feral lout,
Be sure to alert the magistrates
By calling the footpad out.'

The people scattered, went to their homes
And locked and bolted each door,
Then stood there parting the curtains,
Just to be safe and sure,
Most of the men were still at work
But not for the widow Hayes,
She'd not long buried the husband
She'd loved in her salad days.

So when she turned the key in the lock
She couldn't resist a tear,
She missed the man who would hold her hand
And quieten every fear,
She was much too young for a widow,
Or that's what everyone said,
And so was Tom, but he'd travelled on,
Had left to lie with the dead.

She turned, was suddenly listening
When she heard an alien note,
And there stood a man in her kitchen
Holding a knife at her throat,
'I mean no harm, don't be alarmed
I just need a place to stay,
And please don't weep, for I just need sleep,
But don't give the game away.'

He made her lie on her narrow bed
And he cuddled up behind,
One of his arms around her waist
Though he asked if she didn't mind,
She lay there, feeling his body warmth
And it made her think of Tom,
Would ever she feel like this again,
How long, Oh Lord, how long?

She didn't know how it happened, but
She felt when he raised her shift,
Deep in the dark, dead pit of night
Her skirt had begun to lift,
She bit her knuckle and shed the tears
That would soak her pillowcase,
And muttered, when it was over, 'So,
That's what they mean by rape!'

She cooked him a meal at breakfast time
And thought, 'He isn't so bad.'
Then, 'What if my folks could see me now,
They'd think I was going mad.
I'm cooking a meal for a murderer
Though he says that it wasn't him,
He thinks that it was his neighbour
So he says, some guy called Jim.'

He stayed three days and was gone that night,
Under a starless sky,
The widow Hayes had grown fond of him,
It was hard to say goodbye.
But the news came back that they cornered him
Had seen him try to escape,
And questioned what she had done with him,
She didn't mention the rape.

They sent him down at the old Assize,
And sentenced him for his crime,
They wouldn't believe that it wasn't him
'They say that, all of the time!'
He struggled up on the gallows there
With the face of a man who begs,
While she stood near in the Hanging Square,
Stepped up, and pulled on his legs.

The Hammer of Thor

I used to think that thunder was
The sound of the Hammer, Thor,
He'd beat it up on the clouds above
Each time he was waging war,
He'd quell his foes with a lightning strike
Or drown them all in his rain,
Whenever he came along at night
His purpose was always pain.

For we lived down in the valley where
The tendency was to flood,
Whenever the river was swollen with
A squirt of his enemy's blood,
We'd have to climb up to higher ground
And sit there, soaked to the skin,
With lightning flashing around our heads
We'd need to pay for our sins.

'Pay for our sins,' my father said
In a voice that rumbled and roared,
He'd pull a hood up over his head
And speak to the god called Thor,
Then Thor replied with a mighty blast
To drown out my father's cries,
As if he answered him there at last,
'All that you speak are lies!'

While mother sat in a silent weep
As often she'd done before,
'Why did you have to build our house
Way down on the valley floor?
We would have been safer, further up
And still walk down to the stream,
To carry a bucket of water up,
But all that you do is dream!'

That was his sin, my mother said,
He didn't know black from white,
He never looked far enough ahead
He didn't know wrong from right,
Dreaming up schemes that failed, it seems
Like a prophet, living in dread,
That one black night at the river's height
We'd all be drowned in our bed.

'Not that his bed means much to him,'
My mother would often moan,
'Not since that gypsy girl, that Kym
Stayed in the valley alone,
He spends his time in her caravan
Drinking her gypsy tea,
And letting her hold and read his hand,
He never did that with me!'

And so it was on a cold, black night
He'd gone to her caravan,
'Just to check that she'll be all right,'
He said, just playing the man,
The thunder crashed on the mountain top
While we prayed, and gave up thanks,
To the mighty Thor beating at our door
That the river not break its banks.

Lightning flashed though the vale of trees
Where she'd parked her gypsy van,
And then my mother was on her knees
As we heard a mighty bang,
For lightning struck at the heart of sin
And it set the van ablaze,
While both the sinners were trapped within
And paid for their sinful ways.

We buried him on the valley floor
For my mother said, 'It's right.
He doesn't deserve a headstone
Nor a grave that's watertight.'
Whenever the god of thunder calls
And the river overflows,
I think of my father down below
And I wonder if he knows.

The End of The Grange

There isn't much left of The Grange today,
There isn't much left at all,
Only a charred left wing, I think,
And the odd, still standing wall,
The central Hall is a pile of ash
As it was, the day I left,
Sat on the back of the doc's grey mare
As the Lady Mary wept.

It wasn't supposed to end like this
On the day of the wedding ball,
Balloons and streamers hung from the roof
As the marriage carriage called,
Annette stepped out like a fairy queen
In her virgin white, and lace,
While Reece, the Groom, in the wedding room
Had a smile on his handsome face.

And I led the Lady Mary in
To the mother's pride of place,
I only had eyes for her that day
As she walked with a widow's grace,
It wasn't a secret, I yearned for her
But this was her daughter's day,
So I was content with the hand she lent
For she squeezed, along the way.

The priest stood up by a lectern as
The guests all prayed and knelt,
To bless their way on this wedding day
I'm sure it was truly felt,
But Mary's brother-in-law was there
With an evil look in his eye,
He'd wanted to claim the Grange from her
Since the day her husband died.

'The Grange belonged to my family,'
He'd say, 'and I want it back,
You only married into the place
When you wed my brother, Jack.'
He made an offer, but she said no,
The Grange had become her home,
'You sold your part to Jack at the start
Before you went off to roam.'

But Douglas, he had an evil mind
And his countenance was stern,
He said if he couldn't have The Grange
Then he'd rather see it burn.
He'd brought three barrels of gunpowder
Unseen, but out in the yard,
He chose this day to make Mary pay,
We should have been on our guard.

The guests were all engaged at the front
When he wheeled the barrels in,
It takes a mind of evil intent
To imagine this kind of sin,
Annette had lifted her wedding veil
And raised her lips to the groom,
When all hell suddenly came to play
In the depths of that wedding room.

The hall was full of the screams and cries
Of those who lay on the floor,
While I picked the Lady Mary up
And carried her out to the door,
It was there we saw the bride, Annette
Who'd made it out to the porch,
The groom was dead, but the bride had fled
As her dress went up like a torch.

There isn't much left of the Grange today,
There isn't much left at all,
Only a charred left wing, I think,
And the odd, still standing wall.
But the Lady Mary married me
In the wake of all the strife,
Her daughter's gone, but our love is strong,
And Douglas is serving life.

Birdsong

There lives a poet beyond the trees
But all that he writes is pain,
He spends his evenings down on his knees
Regretting the way he came,
He thinks of the path he should have trod
And the path that he really took,
Then writes regrets in a verse to God
And places them all in a book.

A single book on an altar there
That nobody else will see,
He won't let anyone read his verse
For, 'That's between God, and me!'
But he reads and writes them over again
And his tears will stain his cheek,
'They're only the faults of mortal men,'
He thinks, but they make him weep.

He weeps for the loss of an innocence
That he barely remembers now,
It seems so long since his world went wrong
Yet he cannot imagine how.
He tried so hard to be godly then
But the good in his deeds went sour,
And hurt so many he knew back when,
He lies in his bed, to cower.

His heart had leapt on the wings of love
It brought him a purer truth,
He thought she came from the lord above
But all that she had was youth,
And time and fortune had withered that
As the tone in her voice went harsh,
It went from roses and sweet perfume
To the croak you hear in the marsh.

Would nothing pleasant inspire his verse,
Would nothing brighten his day?
He'd sit and chew on his feather quill
And search for something to say.
There must be more to a life than this
For others were doing well,
While he would brood on the sadder bits,
Imagining life as hell.

A girl went wandering though the trees
Carolling loud and clear,
It brought the poet up from his knees
And straining so he could hear,
She sang the song of a trilling bird
And the poet's eyes were bright,
His heart leapt higher the more he heard
And he took her home that night.

His verses now hold the sweet refrain
Of a birdsong, light and free,
He wields his quill with an inner thrill,
'How could this happen to me?'
The book of pain on the altar's stained
With neglect, and barely a nod,
'I'll take this life with my darling wife
And I'll leave the rest to God!'

The Battling Ghosts

'You have to come up to the house,' she said,
'I hate to be there at night,
I have two ghosts in the old bedposts
And each of them wants to fight,
They make their way to the kitchen there
And clatter the pots and pans,
The woman ghost is a Gretel, and
The masculine ghost is Hans.'

I said, 'You must be imagining,
There's not a ghost you can see,'
'Well, I've got two and I'm telling you
I see, believe you me!
The guy is a cranky, violent fool,
He must have been bad in life,
While she defends herself with a stool
Each time that he beats his wife.'

The house was Gothic and Romanesque
And leaned out over the street,
It had an arch like a gothic church
With an overhead retreat.
And that's where she kept the poster bed
Where the ghosts, she said, reside,
'They can't come out in the light of day
So they go in there to hide.'

We spent the evening playing cards
To wait for the witching hour,
Sat in our coats to await the ghosts
And their ectoplasmic shower,
'It often gets messy,' Cassandra said,
'At the point they first appear,
They give out this vapour in the air,
A bit like the froth on beer.'

It must have been eleven o'clock
When Cassandra fell asleep,
I thought I could see her nodding off
Though her eyes began to peep,
Each nostril gave out a pale white smoke
And it formed on left and right,
One was Gretel and one was Hans
And it gave me quite a fright.

It didn't take them a moment then,
She screamed and he would bawl,
He beat her with a broom handle and
Then pinned her against the wall,
She kicked him fair in the shins and ran
Right out of the room in there,
I watched him yell as he followed her
Down by the kitchen stair.

And then there was a clatter of pans
A noise like you've never heard,
They threw them around the kitchen
Until Gretel was calling 'Merde!'
I tried to rouse Cassandra, who
Was groggy, but still awake,
I said, 'You'll have to be exorcised,'
And watched her begin to shake.

'They may have been in the bedposts when
You came, I'm sure that's true,
But maybe they found a better place
For now they live in you.'
I told her the ectoplasm formed
From her, and from whence it came,
She covered her mouth and nose and said,
'They'll never get back again!'

When daylight dawned in that gothic house
And the sun came shining in,
The ghosts came back to the bedroom and
They paid for their ghostly sin,
Cassandra fended them off until
They both were shouting, 'Merde!'
Until the light had destroyed them with
A scream that you should have heard.

There's not been a ghost in that gothic house
From then until this day,
I'm visiting still with Cassandra and
We've found a game to play,
It has to do with that poster bed
With its polished, wooden posts,
But the one thing that we're certain of,
We'll never be seen by ghosts.

The Stand-Over Man

He told me that once he'd killed someone,
A long, long time in the past,
He'd held him down and he'd used a gun,
I said I was just aghast.
He said it merely to threaten me,
I don't know if it was true,
He said if I kept on seeing her,
'In future, that could be you!'

He shocked me so that my hands had shook,
I reached and grabbed at his coat,
I said, 'Don't ever dare threaten me
Or you'll feel my hands at your throat!'
His face went white and he backed away
He wasn't the bravest one,
But turned to say as he walked away,
'Next time, I'll carry a gun.'

I asked Joanne if she even knew
Just what he was really like,
She laughed, and said it was said in fun,
'Just tell him to take a hike.'
She'd once gone out on a party date
With him, but only the once,
He seemed to think they were drawn by fate,
'But really, he's such a dunce.'

'Do you think that we should tell the police,
You know, it might have been true,
How would you feel if someone died
And all on account of you?'
'Believe me, he wouldn't have the guts,
He's just a weasel at heart,
Put him next to a skunk, you'll see,
You couldn't tell them apart.'

Joanne and I went our different ways,
It hadn't been working out,
I found her nice but her heart was ice,
That's not what it's all about.
She passed me by with a man called Guy
And I wished them well to begin,
She said that Ted had gone off his head,
Had started his threatening.

It must have been only a month or more
That I heard how Guy was done,
His body lay in the city morgue
After a hit and run.
Joanne was almost beside herself
In fear, and took to her bed,
'It's true, I should have listened to you,
It must have been Ted,' she said.

The Spring had faded to Summer when
I ran into her again,
Clung to the arm of the hated Ted,
I couldn't believe it then.
But the fear was there in her startled eyes
It was all too plain to see,
He looked at me with a faint surprise
And he said, 'Now look at me!'

I wasn't surprised when the news came down
Along with the winter flood,
A woman ran from a house in town
Upset, and covered in blood,
A man lay stabbed in the bed in there
It seems that she'd cut his throat,
She said it was more than a saint could bear
In a hasty, scribbled note.

I don't know what will happen to her
They say it's up to the court,
But I'll be there as a witness for
Joanne, and the justice sought.
She'd known it wasn't an idle threat
When she saw what happened to Guy,
And said that he had her terrified
When he mouthed the word, 'Goodbye!'

The Ceremony

The sun had set on the mountain top
Before we could get away,
I hadn't wanted to drive by night
But rather the light of day,
The sky was filled with a ghostly glow
The last few rays of the sun,
When I drove out to the open road,
Our journey had just begun.

I'd promised that I would get her there
I wasn't going to renege,
She must have asked me a dozen times,
Was even beginning to beg,
I said, 'They're going to be waiting there
No matter how late we are,
They won't be starting without you, girl,
For you are the principle star.'

That calmed her down, she was mollified,
Though she'd been upset for days,
She worried that she'd be there too late,
She'd said, in a blank dismay,
She thought it was such an honour to
Be picked as the chosen one,
'I've never been picked for anything,
Before,' was the song she sung.

We nosed down into the valley as
The darkness turned to grim,
With only the beam of the headlights
Like a tunnel we were in,
'It seems to be taking a lifetime,'
Was the only thing she said,
'I know, but the end of a lifetime is
The time that you are dead.'

She'd paid especial attention to
The dress she had to wear,
Had glossed her lips and had rouged her cheeks
And had tidied up her hair,
I paid her the best of compliments
That I knew she wanted to hear,
And told her that I was proud of her,
On this special night of the year.

We finally came to a grove of trees
And we turned our headlights in,
Throwing fantastic shadows as our
Wheels began to spin,
We stopped just under a giant oak
And I said, 'We're here at last.
You're certain you want to go through with it?'
She said, 'It will be a blast!'

Then shapes came out of the grove of trees
Wearing hoods and capes of black,
They gathered around the car, and stood
And stared, on that forest track,
When Emily went to join them they
Stood back to let her pass,
And led her into a clearing where
She lay down, on the grass.

It was then they began their chanting
Like a choir in a church,
Rising and falling, lilting, it was fine
And yet a dirge,
For then a man danced into the ring
Who wore the head of a goat,
From under his cape he drew a knife,
Leant down, and cut her throat.

The Message that Did Me Harm

I've often received weird messages,
Nothing to do with me,
They come through the cyber passages
So called, that would set you free,
But then came one with an evil turn
It scuttled on out, then hid,
Accusingly, it appeared to me
And said, 'I know what you did!'

Just that, 'I know what you did,' it said,
And nothing much more than that,
I had no idea just what it meant
It had just popped up, in chat.
There wasn't a name, there wasn't a face
To tell me who it was from,
I tried at first to ignore it, but
It dropped on me like a bomb.

In short, my friends had received the note
And saw it addressed to me,
It seems it had gone my contacts round
And roused curiosity,
For over the next few days they all
Called in, just one by one,
Asking the same thing, overall,
'Just what was it that you've done?'

Of course, I replied in every case
'I really haven't a clue,
People make accusations but
It doesn't mean they are true.'
It was then that the evil jokes began
For some of them like to kid,
To me, it wasn't so funny when
They asked, 'Where's the body hid?'

I snapped on back, 'Get serious!'
I wasn't at all impressed,
'How would you feel if this was you,
Do you think you'd be distressed?'
For some of my so-called 'friends' it seems
My answer raised their ire,
For more than one called a smoking gun,
And 'There's no smoke without fire!'

I felt determined to let it go,
To ignore the joke, at least,
But then appeared on my Facebook page
The Internet Police.
They said, 'We need to investigate,
A complaint's been made of you,'
I sent them back, 'It's a veiled attack
And it certainly isn't true.'

But the police came round, kicked in my door,
And started to search the place,
Acting like thugs, they tore apart
What little I had of grace.
They packed my only computer up
To cart it out to their van,
That stood outside on the pavement like
I was a wanted man.

'What do you want my computer for,
I need it to use for work.'
'You'll get it back when we've checked it out
If you're not a total jerk.
You might be a dangerous pedophile,
It's evidence that we seek,
If not, then after we search your files
You'll get it back next week.'

The neighbours were gathered around the van
With a scandal in their sights,
They knew that something was going down
That I must have been got to rights.
They pointed fingers and muttered low
In delight, this was a treat,
And for days they stared, and I despaired
When they spat at me in the street.

It matters not if you're innocent,
It matters not if you cry,
Nobody listens to what you say
They mutter, 'Deny, deny.'
Your name is suddenly tainted when
A finger points at you,
Forever you will be painted with
The words, 'What did you do?'

I finally got my PC back
And it didn't take a week,
But not a word of apology
Though I found that revenge is sweet.
They sacked the Police Commissioner
And I'm sure that it wasn't fun,
When someone wrote on his Facebook page
'I know just what you've done!'

The Kiss

'Why would I even look at you?'
She said, when I made my bid,
She must have been all of thirty four,
While I was just a kid.
'I only have eyes for you,' I said,
'That's just the way that it is,
I lie awake in my bed at night
And dream of just one kiss.'

Her hands had fluttered, waved me away,
She was flattered, nevertheless,
I knew, because the way that she turned
Flared out the hem of her dress,
Her legs were fine, and smooth and strong
With shape to her calves and thighs,
I stared at them, though I knew it wrong,
They were candy for my eyes.

'You're far too young for the likes of me,'
She said, a gleam in her eye,
'You're half my age, you're seventeen
So I'll have to say goodbye.'
'I never think about age,' I said,
'I think about looks and grace,
And you have plenty of both,' I said,
'You have a beautiful face.'

She laughed then, showing her gleaming teeth
And the dimple in each cheek,
Her lips were crimson, egging me on
I could have stared at her for a week.
'You do go on,' were the words she said
But her cheeks began to flush,
While I was thinking of her in bed,
And that brought a sudden hush.

'I really think you are serious,'
She said, as if in surprise,
'Never more sure and certain,' then
I caught the look in her eyes.
'Maybe if you were twenty-one,
I might just give it a whirl,'
'I'm old enough and I'm full of love,
To me, you're only a girl.'

I reached on out and I held her hand,
The palm of her hand was wet,
I sensed that here was the promised land
I might be successful yet.
And then in a moment's madness she
Had raised her face to my lips,
And heaven opened before me as
She gave me just one kiss.

The Widow Crope

She cooked the final meals at the gaol,
Collected the hangman's clothes,
For he inherited everything
Of the hanged man, heaven knows.
She gave the widows the twist of rope
That he'd used to hang their men,
It all came down to the widow Crope
And whether she liked you, then.

She'd interview the widow-to-be
With a questionnairre or two,
About her man, was he handy, and
What did he like to do?
Then later, in the condemned man's cell
She'd say that she'd cut him free,
'You'll never see your woman again,
So all you have left is me.'

Her husband had died on the gallows, so
She'd known of that final grope,
A widow Kerr had done it for her
Before she was widow Crope.
Then down beneath that terrible drop
She would wait for him to appear,
Hang on his feet, as well as not
While he kicked at the air in fear.

Then once that the corpse was pale and still
She'd take it down to the morgue,
Lay it out on a slab, and then
She'd borrow the gaoler's sword.
And while they were pouring the candlewax
For a later hanging in chain,
She'd slice a couple of fingers off
For the rings that were hers to claim.

But then she might, in an act of spite
Cut off a dead man's hand,
Dip it well in the candlewax
And walk it late through the land.
She'd light the end of the fingertips
And carry it like a torch,
Making her way where the widow lay
And spike it, out on her porch.

And wives would say as their husbands lay,
'Don't mess with the widow Crope,
If ever the hangman comes, that day
She may be your final hope.'
And those awaiting a capital case
Would sit with their husbands there,
And tell them that it would be okay
In that final act of despair.

She'd never worn anything else but black,
She called them her widows weeds,
But never, she said, felt safe from attack
For her husband's evil deeds,
She finally married the hangman, Jed,
And handed the job to her,
An hour since she'd hung on his legs
And made her the widow Claire.

The Bad Timekeeper

They'd shovelled her husband into the ground
Before she got to the grave,
She wasn't able to keep good time
And her husband used to rave:
'I spend my life, waiting for you,
You'll be late for your funeral,'
That wasn't due, but it may come true,
She was late for his, do tell!

He wasn't a very pleasant man
He was known for his violent moods,
She'd married the guy, then wondered why,
He was often downright rude.
She knew what he was capable of
For he'd often flipped his lid,
And left a trail of destruction then
For that was the thing he did.

If only she had got to the grave
In time for a swift goodbye,
And with a spray, sent him away,
She may have just heard him sigh.
But he must have known she was still at home
When the hearse, with him inside,
Arrived at the local cemetery
On time, but without his bride.

She lay awake in the bed that night
And thought she could hear him breathe,
Just across from her pillowcase
And her breast began to heave.
The wind sough-soughed at the windowsill
And she heard a step on the stair,
She wished for once she had been on time
To know she had left him there.

But she hadn't seen the coffin drop
And the hole was almost full,
She'd asked that they uncover it
But she didn't have the pull.
She only hoped he was six feet down
Unable to get back out,
When there was a rattle, out on the porch
And she heard a dead man shout.

'Late, you're late, you're always late,'
It moaned, in an eerie tone,
'You couldn't get to the grave on time
So you left me all alone.
You'd not come even to say goodbye
And for that, you'll pay the price,
For I'll reach out of the grave tonight
And I promise, it won't be nice!'

The shutters began to rattle and bang
And the door flew out, ajar,
The wind howled in like a taste of sin
'I know just where you are!'
She shrieked, and pulled the covers up
And placed them over her head,
'You just can't stay, please go away,
You can't be here, you're dead!'

The covers were torn from her huddled form
And from what the coroner said,
'Her face was white, she died of fright,'
Curled up in her lonely bed.
There was just one thing in the autopsy
That was missed, and he made a note,
The thing was botched, for her husbands watch
He found, was lodged in her throat.

The Revenge of Elsie Hood

He looked on down from the higher ground
At the village he held in thrall,
A gaggle of bowers, of steeples and towers
And he ruled them, overall.
They went their way each enchanted day
Unknowingly bound in his spell,
Not able to leave, to fret or to grieve
While he ruled their wishing well.

The wishing well in the village square
That had been since ancient days,
Nobody knew who put it there
Some sage with enchanted ways,
Its spirit was always known for good
Till they dragged her from a ditch,
That haggard harridan, Elsie Hood,
Known as the village witch.

They'd ducked her once in the village pond
To see if the crone would float,
Pricked her skin with many a pin
So the Witch Finder could gloat,
The sentence passed was the first and last
For a witch, in that village dell,
While some were stern, said a witch should burn,
She was tossed, head first down the well.

The well grew an ugly, creeping moss
That gave off an evil smell,
And everything good from it was lost
Some said, 'It's the witches spell!'
Then he had come to the village square
And tossed in a coin or two,
Said, 'I command, let me rule the land
And the village surrounding you.'

And from that day they were cut away
From the villages all around,
Each road would twist with an evil mist
They were lost, and not to be found,
While he looked down from the higher ground
To gloat on each church and bower,
For then by stealth he had taxed their wealth
Though all that he had was power.

A maiden sat in the village square
Selling her flowers and blooms,
Each day, enchanting the people there
By night, in the Tavern's rooms,
She caught his eye, and he breathed a sigh
When she smiled, so innocently,
So he went to tell the wishing well
'That's who I want, for me!'

The spirit flew from the wishing well,
The spirit of Elsie Hood,
'I've done the thing that you want me to,
But now you want her, for good!'
It dragged him screaming across the square,
And tore at his eyes and skin,
His blood was spread almost everywhere
By the time that she dropped him in.

The mist has gone, it has moved along
The roads in and out are clear,
The moss dried up on the wishing well
And the girl, well she's still here.
They filled the well to the top with sand
So no-one conjures a spell,
They'd rather be part of the greater land
Than wish in a wishing well.

Against All Odds

She lived in a tiny cottage
On top of a sea-bound bluff,
Looked down on the cold blue waters
In fair weather, and in rough,
The smoke that curled from her chimney piece
Was snatched away by the wind
So couldn't obscure the window where
She stood, and her eyes were pinned.

She saw the gaggle of soldiers
Rise up, and out of the marsh,
And remembered a past encounter,
Their treatment of her was harsh,
She snipped the lock on the window, then
She hurried to bar the door,
Raised the trap to the cellar, and
Slid down to the cellar floor.

She lay in hopes they would pass on by,
Would ignore her humble home,
Would think that there was a man nearby
Not a woman there, alone,
She knew of the fate of others who
Had invited the soldiers in,
For many a soldier's bairn was born
The result of a soldier's sin.

She heard them muttering round the house
And tapping the window pane,
Beating a tattoo on the door
Till she thought she'd go insane,
They'd seen the smoke from her chimney piece
And they called, 'Hey you inside,
We need to shelter the night at least,
It's wintry here outside.'

But still she lay on the cellar floor
As quiet as any mouse,
She wasn't going to let them in
To her tiny little house,
She heard the crash as the timber gave
Away on her cottage door,
And heard the thump of their feet above
As they stomped across her floor.

She heard the sound of their puzzlement
When they found the cottage bare,
'Somebody must have lit the fire,
But now, they're just not there.'
She heard them smashing her crockery
And drinking beer from her pot,
She never had enough food to spare
But she knew they'd eat the lot.

Down below was a musket that
She'd kept well oiled and cleaned,
Along with a horn of powder that
She'd felt worthwhile redeemed,
She found the shot and she rammed it home
There was nothing left to chance,
The first to open that trapdoor would
Begin his final dance.

The night came on and they settled down,
Above, she could hear them snore,
She wondered whether they'd go away
When the sun came up, once more,
But then, sometime in the early hours
She heard the trapdoor creak,
And a pair of eyes were hypnotised
As they saw the musket speak.

There once was a tiny cottage
On top of a sea-bound bluff,
It's now burnt out, just a shell without
A roof or a door, it's rough,
While down in the cold blue waters
Lies a woman, drowned and dead,
And up on the bluff, a soldier's grave,
Buried, without a head.

Overboard

They'd all been swept to the beach and left
Like flotsam, after the storm,
Some were alive and some were dead
In that tragic scene, at dawn,
Their ship was lying submerged out there
While its mast still graced the sky,
Its time was brief on that unmarked reef,
Out where its bones would lie.

While those who had been swept overboard
Into a foam-fleck'd sea,
Were helpless, dashed by the giant waves
On rocks that they couldn't see,
They tore the flesh from the living bone
And crushed the skull as they hit,
The sea was turning a muddy red
With blood that was lost in it.

Then when the tide had come churning in
With its charnel bodies and bones,
Above the roar of the rabid shore
You could hear the first few moans,
A sailor lay with a broken arm
Another nursing his head,
And there a woman, so frail of form,
Who certainly should be dead.

She lay with her skirt around her waist,
Her legs were a mass of blood,
Dragged and tossed on a needle rock
She'd suffered more than she should,
But though she moaned she had looked around
As the bodies came floating in,
'Where *are* you Alan A-Dell,' she cried,
'To lose you now is a sin.'

But Alan A-Dell was still out there
The waves would pummel and pound,
He had no thought of the girl that called
As he floated there, face down,
The love they'd shared was a mystery
That had held them wrapt in awe,
But now had passed into history
As he floated in, to the shore.

And Carmel cried as the rising tide
Kept sweeping the bodies in,
For Alan A-Dell now lay beside
The lover that once had been,
She thought of the final words he'd said
As they both jumped into the waves,
'I pray, if there is a God above,
That you are the one he saves.'

And so she wept as she beat his chest
And railed at the living God,
'Why take half of a love away
When a love takes two, that's odd.'
The sun burst suddenly through the clouds
And it made the water gleam,
As Alan A-Dell had spluttered once
His body and life redeemed.

They clutched each other that livelong day
Alone on that charnel beach,
Everyone else had died, they lay
Where living was out of reach,
The night came down on that lonely shore
With no-one to help or care,
So shivered into the early hours
When suddenly, God was there.

He hadn't taken a single love
She'd said that a love takes two,
So looking down from his place above
He knew what he had to do,
And when they died in each others arms
With their hearts within them stilled,
A love was taken, not one, but two,
With his grace, their love was sealed.

Jabuka

It stood by my uncle's hatstand for
As long as I can recall,
This ugly wooden carving, leering
Staring out from the wall,
My mother would say, 'It's evil,'
That it wasn't fit to see,
Not for a young impressionable,
By that, she just meant me.

It used to give me the shivers
Every time that I passed its way,
It had a glare of malevolence
I felt, in a mute dismay,
My uncle brought it from Africa
A memento of his time
Seeking out the Azuli tribe
Who lived in a tropic clime.

'I think his name was Jabuka,'
My uncle said to a friend,
'One of those baleful spirits that
Was said to torture men,
He'd pluck your eyes from their sockets
If you saw what you shouldn't see,
And infected men with a virus
That would kill their family.'

For years it sat in abeyance,
Whatever the power it bore,
There was never a hint of impatience
As it sat, and stared by the door,
It wasn't until my uncle hired
A sultry African maid,
That evil entered the atmosphere
Of the house where I went, and played.

I think it was then that I noticed
There was something strange at large,
My hair rose up as I walked on by,
An electrostatic charge,
It prickled in all my fingers
Ran up the hairs of my arm,
I'd lie if I should deny that day
I felt a sense of alarm.

While little dark skinned Mbutu,
Would bow when she'd dust it off,
Would mumble some words in Zulu
That I could make nothing of,
I saw the fear in her eyes the day
I glanced off it in the hall,
'Never to touch Jabuka, son
Or him rage is fearful!'

It must have been close on midnight
I heard, when over and done,
My uncle came on Mbutu
Stark naked before 'the one',
It must have been some strange African rite
As she danced, she gave weird cries,
But then next day, my uncle lay
And bled from both of his eyes.

My aunt then died of Ebola,
No more than a week from then,
The virus grew, then Mbutu too
Was lost to the world of men,
I sat by my uncle's bedside
At the hospital by the park,
When he said, 'Oh Ben, I'm a fool,' and then,
'God, but this room is dark!'

He told me to take Jabuka
And carry it out that day,
'But while you carry that evil thing
Be sure you're looking away,
There's petrol out in the potting shed,
Though barely a gallon or two,
Make sure you douse it over the head,
You know what you have to do.'

I watched the flames as they roared and claimed
The wood of that idol's gaze,
And felt the surge of an evil urge
Attack, in so many ways,
I knew I'd watched what I shouldn't see
As I felt it rise in my hair,
And lost one eye as it bled bone dry,
It's lucky I have a spare!

Not Enough...

She left without any warning,
Not even saying goodbye,
I turned around and she'd gone to ground
And I always wondered why.
It's not that I didn't love her,
And not that I showed no care,
But I got up in the morning
And I found she wasn't there.

I didn't know where to find her
There wasn't even a note,
The only thing that she'd said to me
About leaving was, I quote:
'I can't see a long-term future,
I can't see an always 'us',
There'll come a day when I want away
And I'd hate to make a fuss.'

I noticed her empty wardrobe
For the door she left ajar,
She'd taken the quilt, her drawers were spilt
And she took our second car,
I drove around to her friend's address
And I asked where she had gone,
But she accused me of carelessness
For losing her friend, Yvonne.

The house is suddenly cold and dark
For she failed to pay the bill,
A dreadful silence is on my heart
For I love the woman still,
And clouds have gathered since she has gone
There's rain upon the step,
I didn't think I would feel the chill
But I find my eyes are wet.

It's not as if I can plead my case
For I don't know where she is,
The world's a cruel and empty place
When you lose a goodnight kiss,
Perhaps she's gone to another love
Is the thought that drives my fear,
Then what I offered was not enough
At the turning of the year.

The Ancient City of Lon

We went down in the submersible
Just Andy Malone and me,
The project wasn't reversible
Beneath the Andaman sea,
The funding for it a one-time off
So we needed to get it done,
To investigate the sunken state
Of the ancient city of Lon.

We knew it was there from a sonic probe
That had mapped the sunken bed,
Five centuries it had been down there
From the documents we'd read,
There were buildings, markets, standing still
And a huge cathedral dome,
We needed to take some photographs
To show to the folks back home.

It was over a thousand fathoms deep
So the pressure was intense,
With systems go, the descent was slow
And it kept us in suspense,
We wondered how it had got down there
How the land had slipped away,
To carry a city so deep with what
Had once comprised a bay.

The beam of the single searchlight pierced
Its way through the deepening murk,
The further that we descended meant
We were peering into the dark,
But then at a thousand fathoms we
Caught sight of the massive dome,
It was almost like the cathedrals that
Had once been built back home.

With cameras flashing furiously
We continued our descent,
Noting the gaps where windows once
Had peered on out at Lent,
But we didn't think it was christian
For the Hindu figures swarmed
Over the outer surfaces
Where once, the sun had warmed.

The beam had picked out an archway then
With the entrance from a porch,
Some of the pillars had fallen in
And the doors were gone from the arch,
We headed into the darkened space
Our light picked out in the gloom,
And chills were rippling up my spine
As we entered that darkened room.

We floated in and along the aisle
Where the pews were made of stone,
It had the eeriest feeling like
We weren't in there alone,
And at the end was an altar stood
As it had, five hundred years,
And by its side was a figure crouched
Or the bones of a figure, cursed.

The searchlight gave it an eery glow
As we turned and travelled back,
There was something strange about that thing
For all the bones were black,
And lying flat on the altar stone
Was a weird and evil gleam,
A blade rose up from a corpse on that
But the bones were white and clean.

'They must have been making a sacrifice
At the moment disaster struck,'
Said Andy, as we peered on out,
And he turned to take a look,
The crouching figure began to rise
In the current our craft had spawned,
And in the beam we could see the gleam
Of a perfect pair of horns.

It seemed that it reached on out to us
With its bony fingers raised,
It appeared to point to Andy who
Screamed out, like someone crazed,
I heard a thump and I turned to him
Just as my partner fell,
All burned and black as his flesh had peeled
In a vision straight from hell.

I headed the craft toward the arch
In a panic, I confess,
My friend lay dead and I lost my head
And I think you'd not do less,
I left that place in a burning haste
With its devil crouched once more,
Back and beside that altar stone
It will stay forevermore.

They said it must be a power short
That had burned and killed my mate,
But I said, 'Look at the pictures, you
Will see the face of hate,'
Of one thing I can be certain now
That the funding all has gone,
There's no-one keen to explore once more
The ancient city of Lon.

The Mangling Hook

There must have been seven chimneys
In the great house on the hill,
I never actually counted them
While the house was standing still,
But the years had brought their own neglect
And the house was well run down,
By the time we pulled the place apart
For a new estate in town.

We couldn't just use a wrecking ball
It was too immense for that,
When we took it brick by brick apart
We could build a hundred flats.
The chimneys were the hardest part
For the flues had twists and turns
As they rose up through three storeys with
Each hearth, soot black and burned.

It had been the home of Dukes and Earls
Back in Victoria's day,
With gardeners, cooks and pantry maids,
All with a place to stay,
There were balls and more for the gentlefolk
For the vicar and local squire,
And after the garden parties they would
Huddle, in front of the fire.

We chipped away at the chimney stacks
And gradually brought them down,
Brick by brick to the local tip
As red dust covered the ground,
But then a guy gave a sudden cry
During a working lull,
'I think I see, what it seems to me,
The top of a human skull.'

The top of a human skull it was
Of a child, no more than six,
Jammed up tight in the chimney there
Imprisoned by old red bricks,
We managed to pry him loose at last
And lifted him from the flue,
But then the horror came home to us
For his legs were missing, too.

We saw the mangling hook they'd used
That lodged in one of his ribs,
That tore the body apart to clear
The chimney, for His Nibs,
The kid was lodged in a twisting flue
They knew that his case was dire,
And tried to make him climb up and through
By lighting a smoking fire.

We couldn't tell if the sweep was dead
Or simply allowed to choke,
When someone ordered the fire lit
And sent up a cloud of smoke,
Perhaps he screamed as the smoke had streamed
And the fire burned, but slow,
He was just a sweep, his life was cheap
Compared to the guests below.

The little lad's in the cemetery
He was laid with special care,
With everyone but nobility
Gathered to lay him there,
It's a page at last from a cruel past
That we turned, but won't forget,
Great wealth destroys our humanity,
Have we learned that lesson yet?

Mirror Image

The mirror was there when we moved in,
Full length, and stood in the hall,
Right where the lounge room opened up
Against the opposite wall.
Yvette was startled at first, she said,
'That mirror gave me a fright,
To see a figure suddenly there
Stare back in the dead of night.'

'You'll soon get used to it there, Yvette,
There's nowhere else it can go,
Once you have moved your chattels in
And filled up the house below.'
'It's strange though, isn't it,' said Yvette,
'It reflects the wrong way round,
My right is left and my left is right
Like an opposite me it's found.'

'You'd better tell her you're not impressed,
That she's taken half your face,
And moved it to the opposite side
In a sign of twisted grace.'
For Yvette had one green eye, the right,
And a pale blue eye, the left,
So what stared back from that mirror there
Was a back to front Yvette.

She'd stand in front of that mirror there
And would pose, and raise her hand,
'I raise my right, and it seems to me
I'm reversed in mirror land.'
I said, 'It's the same for everyone
But you seem to be obsessed,'
'It isn't me,' said Yvette, 'you'll see
When she steps out through the glass.'

I woke at night, in the early light
And Yvette was not in bed,
I found her down by the mirror there
Where the morning light was shed.
I crept up slowly behind her there
And saw what Yvette could see,
That figure, facing away from her,
But never a sign of me.

'I told the woman to turn around
And she did, I see my back!'
But so did I, it was such a shock
Like a brought-on heart attack,
Yvette went missing the following day
Though I searched both high and low,
But didn't stare at the mirror there
Just in case she was… you know!

I called her name when the evening came
And she crawled right into bed,
'You scared me out of my mind,' I cried,
'But I don't know why,' she said.
She gave me a long, fulfilling kiss
When I stared, as one bereft,
For this Yvette had a blue eye, right
And a green one on the left.

Holy Smoke!

He laid no claim to a perfect life,
Nor looked to a higher power,
'He lived his life,' said his seventh wife
'At a hundred miles an hour.'
And those he bruised as he hurtled by
Were the first in defending him,
'He didn't live by our man-made rules
But those he defined within.'

There were some that said he was selfish,
And some that said he was cruel,
Those with the backward collar he
Devoured, and used as fuel.
He couldn't stomach the hypocrite,
The ones that would have you pray,
'If there is a god, I'll give you the nod,
You wouldn't be here today.'

There wasn't a woman could tame him down
Not a concubine, nor a wife,
He wore out many an eiderdown
In living a lustful life.
He lived as the rest of us should live
In a type of joyful surge,
And carried us all along with him
With our inhibitions purged.

He set a pace that would burn him out
As his strength and youth declined,
But railed and ranted against the force
That made him a prey to time.
'I'll not give in, it would be a sin
To deny in my final breath,
A life that's sailed too close to the rail,
That's an ignominious death.'

He swore that he'd find a way to show
That death only set you free,
As he laid his head on that final bed,
Here's what he said to me:
'Just watch that picture over the hearth
Of me, when the world was young,
I'll make it fall from the chimney wall
If the sting of my death's undone.'

And so he died in his earthly pride
Then went to his funeral pyre,
I told my wife, 'there's another life
Devoured in the flames and fire.'
I didn't believe that he could survive
On the strength of his will alone,
But went away to the wake that day
They held in his childhood home.

His friends were milling about the house
And drinking his cellar dry,
While I stood pensive before the hearth
And asking the question, why?
When a sudden crash on the cobbled hearth
Saw his picture fall from the wall,
The shattered glass from his grinning face
Went showering over all.

It must have been a coincidence
I said, and the wife agreed,
'We'll have to go to the cemetery
To prove that he's there, indeed.'
We waited just on a week to go,
It rained, and the grave was soaked,
But pouring out from his headstone there
Was a plume of Holy Smoke!

The Lazy Eye

She walked the cobblestone streets at night,
Everyone thought her a pro,
Her skirt was short and her blouse was tight
And her eyes moved to and fro,
She never answered a mocking call
For a price to rest her head,
And wouldn't stop till the Moon went down
When at last she went to her bed.

She'd roamed the alleyways and the streets
For a year, or maybe two,
Whenever a stranger stayed her feet
She'd say, 'Not looking for you!'
But still she'd roam till she turned for home
Each night, it went to a plan,
She'd check each face for a sign of grace,
Each night, she'd look for a man.

Sometimes she'd stop at a village Inn
And she'd sidle up to the bar,
The barman said, 'No, you can't come in,'
Then she'd say, 'I've come so far.
I need to know if you've seen a man
With a head of bright red hair,
A lazy eye, with a look quite sly,
I've been searching here and there.'

But no-one knew of the lazy eye
Though they'd seen the carrot head,
'He used to drink at 'The King and I'
But I think that fellow's dead.'
She wandered out to the cemetery
To look for the name they gave,
But the headstone said it was Henry,
When the name that she sought was Dave.'

She'd go back home and she'd cry at night
When the stranger came in her dream,
She'd only seen him the once before
But his face was burnt on her brain.
'I'll not be rid of him, nevermore,
And I'll spend my life in pain,
I need to see him, if just once more,'
It drove her out in the rain.

One night she walked through an alleyway
In shadows, deep in the gloom,
Hiding a figure standing there
Who stared, like a figure of doom.
He faced her there in the only light,
The Moon, that beamed through the trees,
And she took note of the lazy eye
And the hair, like a red disease.

'I think I've seen you before,' he said,
I just can't remember when.'
'You did, while I was lying in bed,
You came through my window then.
I've searched for you for a year or more
And now is your time to pay,
You won't be getting away this time,
So down on your knees, and pray.'

She pulled a pistol out of her bag
To point it at straight at his head,
The stranger's knees had begun to sag,
'I should have left you for dead!'
'I'm glad that your hair is red, blood red,
For the sight won't make me cry,'
Then fired a bullet, straight through his head
By way of his lazy eye.

The Ups and Drowns of Waterdown

Whenever the rain comes falling,
It rearranges our town,
Whatever before was dry and up
Is suddenly wet and down,
They say it's the fault of Widow Krupp
Who saved her tears in a tub,
And splashes them out with a scream and shout
As rain fills the gutters up.

And the streets lie under the waterways
For the river will burst its banks,
Flooding the gardens, and pathways,
There's nobody else to thank.
We lose all sense of the North and South
As the East and West drift by,
And watch as the town goes spinning round
By gazing up at the sky.

People go drifting out in boats
To look for the supermart,
But all they find are the floating goats
That litter the flooded park,
The wooden houses meander by
As they leave their place in the street,
And neighbours wake in a different place
To the one where they fell asleep.

No wonder they call it 'Waterdown'
It could have been 'Waterup',
For Waterdown is a drifting town
Thanks to the Widow Krupp,
The townsfolk threaten to duck the witch
As soon as they find the pond,
That lies bewitched by a flooded ditch
Out there, the back of beyond.

The pub has been anchored down with ropes
To stop it drifting away,
They towed it down from the heart of town
To give them somewhere to play,
While Madame Loy is the local toy
Who hangs her shingle outside,
'Come in and play, if you're bored today,
Entrée, and come for a ride.'

They finally got to the Widow Krupp
And drowned the witch in her tears,
Ducked her well in her wooden tub
Now it hasn't rained for years.
The ground is dry and they wonder why
The river is just a stream,
And for those few who are newly new,
The past was a fitful dream.

The Mirror of Truth

She was everything I ever wanted,
Petite, with a shock of hair,
A dimpled cheek, and a smile so sweet
And my favourite name of Claire.
I'd watched her grow to adulthood
And thought that I'd made my mark,
Until the day that my world turned grey
When I saw her walk in the park.

For she wasn't alone by the cedars,
She wasn't alone by the pool,
For Edward Eyre had his arm round her,
A fellow I'd known at school,
He wasn't exactly a heartthrob,
His eyes were too big for his nose,
His hair was like a rats nest in there
And he seemed too small for his clothes.

I couldn't believe I was seeing
Her laughing and smiling with him,
At school we'd called him the village fool
An idiot under his skin,
But here he was with my darling,
The vision was somehow grotesque,
As I recalled how he once had crawled
Under the teacher's desk.

It wasn't as if he could smell too good
With the egg stains over his chest,
A shirt would have been an improvement,
But he wore a dirty old vest.
What on God's earth could she see in him
I made up my mind to see,
To question Claire, what went on in there,
And what did she think of me?

Her words were a revelation,
To her he was handsome and tall,
But she was barely just five foot three
And he only five foot small.
She spoke of his wit and his humour,
She said he made her heart full,
Then what of me, and she said, 'Let's see,
I think you're remarkably dull.'

I said she should see a psychiatrist
Perhaps an optometrist too,
'For what you see is a travesty
That nobody sees but you.'
She said they were going to be married,
To tie them together for life,
'But once you see what the others see,
You'll make him a terrible wife.'

I went to their wedding reception,
And hung in the passageway hall,
Got Claire to see his reflection
In the mirror that hung on the wall,
She blanched, and gasped at his image,
She'd not seen him like that before,
She'd seen but dreams, and she grimaced,
Threw up on the passageway floor.

There are those who see what they want to see
And Claire had been one of those,
They dress their dreams in a web it seems
Made up of the Emperor's clothes.
We've been together a year or so
And try to hang on to our youth,
Whenever reality strikes a pose
We look in the mirror of truth.

The Switch

The woman walked up to the prison gates
But the guard wouldn't let her through,
'We only have room for the prison inmates
There's certainly none for you.'
'But I need to get in, I have to get in,
My love's to be hanged at the dawn,
If you could show pity, show pity for me,
I need one more kiss, then he's gone!'

'You want dispensation, then talk to the judge,
His chambers are only next door,
He's cold and he's heartless, a hard man to budge,
Tell *him* what you're looking for.
He came to the judgement that fastened the noose
Of death round your lover's throat,
There'll not be much pity to see in his eyes
As he watches your lover choke.'

She went to his chambers and knocked at his door,
He opened it up in surprise,
'Why would you come knocking, it's late in the hour?'
'Tomorrow my lover dies!'
'The judgement is given, it can't be reversed,
He's condemned by the law of the land,'
She looked for compassion, his message was terse,
'When he dies, it is by his own hand.'

She quailed at his hardness, went down on her knees,
'I just need to see him once more,
I'm willing to pay with whatever you please,
I'm begging you, down on the floor.'
The judge saw his options and wickedness gleamed
In the eyes of the law of the land,
He offered an avenue by which it seemed
She'd get one more glimpse of her man.

She'd made up her mind to not shrink from the task
That she'd set herself, nor would she slip,
From offering everything that he might ask
For her man was the prow of her ship.
He took his advantage, it was as she'd feared
On the bench of his Chancery Court,
And left with a pass he had signed as he leered
At the precious few moments she'd bought.

The guard let her in where her man was condemned
And he let them alone for a while,
Her urgency stemmed from the moments they hemmed
In between both a kiss and a smile,
The guard noticed nothing amiss when she left
Her tears hidden under her hair,
Not even a glance at the prisoner in rags
Who crouched in the corner in there.

The figure they dragged to the gallows floor
Was weak and unusually soft,
The judge had been waiting to see the despair
He had caused, with the figure aloft.
Then out called the hangman, 'it isn't a man,
You've brought me a woman to hang,'
A woman who'd already cut off her hair
And given her wig to her man.

'Someone shall pay,' cried the judge in his ire,
'I'll not have the law over-ruled.'
'That someone is you when the things that you do
Allow you to rape, and be fooled.'
The judge then had bellowed, 'we'll hang her instead,'
And the hangman had knotted the noose,
She cried as the trap dropped, 'My love is not dead,
And your law is of no further use.'

Lost Legacy

The house, an aristocratic pile
Sat nestled into the hill,
Hidden by trees and bushes, while
It harboured its silence, still.
No outward sign of its infamy,
No clue to the years before,
When men had described it, clinically
As being, itself, at war.

Designed and built by my grandfather
In a late Victorian style,
It had all the trappings of balconies
And of lacework in wrought iron,
The tiles were Italian marble
And the pathways local stone,
My Grandma, Jenny McArdle,
She gave it a heightened tone.

The gentry came for the parties,
They came for the dress-up balls,
I don't remember a time they weren't
Wandering through the halls,
It fretted Jenny McArdle
Who wanted a little peace,
But Jock was a hunting sporting man
And he wanted peace the least.

He'd take his chums to the library
Where they'd play their six card stud,
There were threats and there was bribery
And before too long there, blood,
Then finally, on an ill starred night
That would hit my grandma hard,
Her husband wagered the house she loved
Just once, on a single card.

The moment she heard the house was gone
She flew at their deck of cards,
Split open the heads of more than one
Left acres of glass in shards,
'You'll not be taking my home from me,'
She screamed at the Earl of Vane,
Before she fell from the balcony,
Cursing her husband's name.

And Jock was never the same again
He had to vacate his home,
While Jenny McArdle's blood was still
Staining the local stone,
They say her ghost wouldn't leave the place
And that's why it caught alight,
Once when her shape had leapt in space
From the balcony one night.

And now I sit in the clearing where
That once great house had sat,
Amidst the trees and the sounds of bees
When I'm feeling low, and flat,
That house, it should have been left to me,
I'm the only downward line,
But still I hear when the weather's clear
My grandma's voice, 'It's mine!'

Spontaneous

One minute she's standing before me,
Is stridently screaming her claims,
And then in a moment of horror,
I watch as she bursts into flames.
There isn't a fire around her,
Not even a spark to begin,
But then she erupts in a moment,
The fire bursts out from within.

I've heard that it's happened to others
They burn with a spiritual flame,
Some essence of horror within them
Devouring their body the same,
But nothing will char things around them
It only destroys skin and bone,
Their chairs and their rooms are protected,
It doesn't set fire to their home.

I try to remember what caused it,
What happened to scramble her brain,
What started the turmoil and forced it
To burst out and drive her insane,
The flames started under her eyelids
Then roared in a burst from her throat
It seemed to be something that I did,
It may have been something I wrote.

I don't dare to start a new friendship,
With women I knew from before,
There's always some thing that might end it
With her flaming out on the floor.
She always said I was controlling,
Was cold and was hard, and I am,
But maybe that's why; she's a woman,
And I, thank my stars, am a man.

Fox and Hounds

The hearse set off through the mansion gates
Pulled by a pair of greys,
Stepping high, so they'd not be late
For the church's hymns of praise,
Lord Gordon Knox on the catafalque
Awaiting his final ride,
Just down the hill where the graveyard spilled
And spread on the eastern side.

But staring out from behind the grass,
From between each tree and bush,
There gleamed the beam of a hundred eyes
In a sacred kind of hush,
The word was out it was Gordon Knox
Set to take his pride of place,
And from the woods had come every fox
To afford his lordship grace.

For Gordon had been the Master of
The Aldermaston Hunt,
Had chased them across the countryside
More than a man can count,
But somehow managed to lose the fox
As it turned, became covert,
And often seemed to confuse the hounds
As the fox returned to earth.

Three generations had come and gone
Since the young Amelia Knox,
Had left to walk in the countryside
And found a secluded copse,
The peasants say that she fell asleep
By a well protected earth,
And Reynard Fox had uncovered her
Before she had given birth.

So Raymond was the first of the breed
In a mix of fox and man,
A Knox by name but a fox by shame
When his mother's guilt began,
And when he had a son of his own
He could see that the eyes were sly,
And every fox in the countryside
Could tell him the reason why.

Gordon carried the bloodline on
Though he rode to fox and hounds,
He ruled the hunt with an iron fist
They were hunting in his grounds,
And every time that the quarry went
He would make a lame excuse,
The scent was wrong, or the wind was strong
Or the hounds were far too loose.

And every time that the Master died
And the hearse had trundled by,
The foxes all came out to see,
In a way, they said goodbye,
But Gordon had left no son behind
Just a daughter, Elspeth Knox,
And I heard they'd given up on her
Till they found her in some copse.

The Phone Call

He was sitting alone by the window
In hopes that the phone would ring,
Just as he'd sat there every day
Since she'd disappeared last Spring,
But snow now lay in the gutter,
Was glistening up in the trees,
And his thoughts would stray fom the words he'd pray,
'Won't you please come home, Louise!'

The phone lay stubbornly silent,
The snow untouched in the street,
There wasn't a cart or a tyremark,
Nor even a sign of feet.
The sky was louring grey outside
As it was, the day she went,
He wished he knew, but hadn't a clue
There had been no argument.

He'd thought perhaps she'd been taken,
Had struggled, against her will,
But there'd been no sign of a ransom,
The phone had stayed silent still.
He'd asked her friends in the neighborhood
What she'd said, could they recall?
But all of them said Louise was good,
That nothing stood out at all.

Her clothes still hung in the wardrobe,
And gave off their faint perfume,
As days went by he would sit and cry
Could barely go in the room,
The Police were as good as useless,
Inferred she'd taken a walk,
'She's probably got a new boyfriend,
If only your walls could talk.'

The only clue that he'd ever found
Was a script in a bag she'd left,
He found the word unpronounceable
But strange that the script was kept,
She wasn't a one for keeping things
She said there were bins for that,
She'd thrown out even a friendship ring
And an old and beaten hat.

One day there were footsteps through the snow
Wound up at his own front door,
He raced to open the doorway up
But the footsteps stopped at the floor,
There wasn't a sign they'd gone away,
There wasn't a sign of retreat,
Whoever had come to his front door
Was still out there in the street.

He went back into the study then
And gazed through the sudden rain,
He never knew when the phone rang through
It would cause him so much pain.
A voice intoned, 'If you're on your own,
Sit down, are you Brian Drew?'
And then went on with its dismal song
'I've a message to pass to you.'

'This is the Somerhill Hospice, with
A body, ready to claim,
It's up to you, but it's Louise Drew
She left a note with your name.
She finally died this morning from
That tumour, found on her lung,
We didn't know she was married, though,
That note was under her tongue.'

'She didn't want you to suffer, it
Was better she went away,
She wrote she hadn't told anyone
But came in as Louise Grey.'
Brian's face became bloodless at
The wet footsteps in the hall,
Then took in the silent nothingness,
And threw the phone at the wall.

The Garden Plot

'What's at the end of the garden,'
I would ask my Lisa May,
Each time she came through the garden gate
With that look of pure dismay.
She'd shake her head, 'It's the garden bed,
Overrun with weeds and toads,
I've said before we should move it more
Away from the old crossroads.'

It didn't seem to be logical
To remove a garden bed,
'What difference, if it goes east or west,'
Is what I plainly said.
But Lisa May was intractable
With her fixed ideas and views,
She said she hated the crossroads that
Still ran beside the mews.

I never used to accompany her
I'm not a gardening man,
I tend to let it run riot as
It does, in nature's plan.
But Lisa wanted to tame it, by
Applying stakes and rules,
To straighten this and align with that,
She's one of nature's fools.

I never took her too seriously,
She'd come back and complain,
'Those toadstools seem to be spreading from
The vermin in the lane.'
I didn't know there was vermin so
I said that I'd take a look,
Reluctant, as I was always but
I sighed, put down my book.

We made our way down the garden, and
I noticed that there were toads,
Their croaking seemed to be loudest
From the site of the old crossroads,
And toadstools clustered around the base
Of an ancient weathered post,
As I heard a sound that came from the ground
Like when a victim chokes.

'The mud there seems to be heaving,' said
My naive Lisa May,
She didn't know that the post had been
A gallows in its day.
And felons, hung for a week or so
Were buried at its base,
I hadn't dared to reveal it or
We'd never have bought the place.

'The land's a little unstable here,
I see just what you mean,
Perhaps we can move the garden bed
To the other side of the green.'
But Lisa May wasn't hearing me
For she stood stock still in shock,
She was staring down at the muddy ground
At what I'd thought was a rock.

'That's not a rock, but a skull,' she cried,
And I must admit, it's true,
That skull rose up of a killer
Buried in 1822.
Then Lisa May, who screamed and ran,
Now leaves the garden alone,
So nature's riot has run amok
And the grave is overgrown.

The Woman Who Never Was

I'd seen her coming and going for
A couple of years or more,
Her hair in the wind was blowing
Every time she walked on the shore,
I must admit I was taken in
By her eyes and her lips of gloss,
She made me think of imagined sin
The woman who never was.

She wore the flimsiest blouses that
Were loose, and tied at the waist,
And lived in one of those houses they
Put up in the new estate.
She seemed to delight in teasing me
By wearing her skirts so high,
The slightest gust from a breeze would free
A glimpse of a naked thigh.

She never actually spoke to me
But she'd raise a brow my way,
While I hung over the garden gate
Thinking of what to say,
And soon it became a ritual
She'd pass in the early hours,
Then come again in the afternoon
With her basket full of flowers.

In time I noticed a subtle change
In the way she wore her hair,
She started to pin it back, and then
It didn't seem so fair.
The eyes that had used to tantalise
Became harder, and the gloss
Was fading out on the ruby lips
Of the woman who never was.

I thought I was slowly losing her
But just a little each day,
Nothing would stay the same, I saw
Her slowly fading away,
I said to a friend, 'What's happening,
I have this sense of loss,'
And he replied she was trapped inside,
The woman who never was.

'She doesn't really exist you know,
It's better you let her free,
You've compromised and idealised
Till she thinks, 'I can't be me.'
She may just show if you let her go,
If you don't, you'll count the loss,
She'll stay forever inside you then
The woman who never was.'

I switched her off and I walked the shore,
Went up to the new estate,
Then held my breath and knocked at her door
And I said, 'I know I'm late.'
She looked at me and she smiled, you see,
And she said, 'My name is Roz,
It's been so long I was feeling wrong
Like the woman who never was.'

The Long Wait

The Inn sat down in a hollow,
Deep in a grove of trees,
It sat so far from the road, the yard
Was two feet deep in leaves,
It looked to be well deserted,
Except for a single light,
That poured its glow on the porch below
Late on that fateful night.

I'd looked since I found the Grimoire
Sat up on that dusty shelf,
Written in faded longhand
I couldn't decipher myself,
The ancient scribe in the library
Had helped to decode each line,
And said it spoke of an ancestor
With a similar name to mine.

It mentioned the Seventh Circle Inn
And where it could still be seen,
It lay astray by a country way
Deep in a copse of green,
And Agnes Drue was a name I knew
Though I heard she'd not been found,
After the Mass they held that day
On consecrated ground.

Her coven had raised a spectre
Beside the Inn, in the woods
Near to a marble altar where
An ancient church had stood,
But then it demanded a sacrifice
To give the Devil his due,
And everyone formed a circle then
Apart from my Agnes Drue.

I entered the Inn to find who kept
The Seventh Circle of sin,
I needed to find what happened to
The one who was lost within,
An ancient crone kept the bar in there
Who croaked, 'I know why you're here,
You're far too late for she's at Hell's Gate,
Has been, for many a year.'

I thought that I'd find a clue in there
On the fate of Agnes Drue,
And asked the crone was she on her own,
Would she rather there were two?'
A screech came up from the cellar then
Like the wail of a troglodyte,
The crone went down with a worried frown,
'She only does that at night!'

Then right in the midst of the cellar floor
Was a seaman's wooden chest,
With iron hasps and rusted clasps
And a chain wound round the rest,
I burst it open to shrieks and cries
That seemed to come from within,
And there was the corpse of Agnes Drue
Where the Devil had locked her in.

The staring eyes in her skull had gone
But they seemed to stare the same,
There was no flesh but the woman's dress
Was torn in a rage of pain,
And held in her frightful bony hand
Was a book that she'd scribbled on,
Deep in the dark of her awful tomb,
'I knew! One day you'd come!'

The Watching Tree

My father called it the Watching Tree
For it turned, and swivelled to see,
He'd planted its seed in the winter weather
On top of the grave of Annabelle Feather
Who killed their mother for why, whatever,
Then hung from a hawthorn tree.

The hangman never would cut her free
While she spun and spiralled around,
Her eyes a-bulge on the village gallows
In front of the church they call All Hallows,
While urchins jeered to toast marshmallows
As Annabelle stared at the ground.

My aunts in pinafores hung on her feet
To stretch her neck with the rope,
Her tongue stuck out at least six inches
A rigid perch for the garden finches
Who pop the eyes of the ones they lynches,
Once they've given up hope.

They laid her down in an open grave
The rope wound tight at her throat,
Planted the seeds of the tree above her
Just to remind of the murdered mother
So people be kinder to one another,
Or that's what my father wrote.

The roots of the tree bored into the skull
Of Annabelle, in through her eyes,
Tendrils of thoughts were left forever
Deep in the well of Annabelle Feather
And sent from her eyes to the tree, whatever,
A poisoner never dies.

So still I call it the Watching Tree
For it waits till I'm not around,
Dropping its poisonous leaves whenever
It's cold and bleak in the winter weather,
As black as the heart of Annabelle Feather
Stone cold, and dead in the ground.

Obsession

I'd seen the widow walk back and forth
The length of the village street,
Her veil so black and her dress so long
You'd see neither face nor feet,
She never would speak to anyone
But would simply seem to glide
Within the folds of that mourning dress
Like a slowly ebbing tide.

At first she'd walk at the early dawn
But then she'd be gone by noon,
The light of day would spirit away
Her wandering sense of gloom,
She'd not be seen till the sun went down
When you'd hear the swish of lace,
Catching along the sea wall stone
And whipping around her face.

She never would miss the evening tide
That would bring the fleet back in,
Check every boat that was still afloat
If its catch was full, or thin,
Her only love had gone out one day
With his sails set high to roam,
His boat had floated out in the bay
But he had not come home.

It took a week for the widows weeds
To start to march on the shore,
And no-one dared to look in her face
So deep was the grief she wore,
'I never knew pain like this exists,'
She'd cry, when she was alone,
But over the next few painful weeks
She knew that he'd not be home.

Then she slowly tore off the widow's veil,
She gave up the mourning dress,
I watched her enter the world again
Just as beautiful, no less.
It took me months but I won her round,
I'd kept my scheme afloat,
By hiding away the tools I'd used
To sink her husband's boat.

The Shadow Eater

Their shadows should have stepped side by side
As once they had done before,
But nobody noticed that one had gone
From the boardwalk trace on the floor,
They still paraded, down by the beach
At the height of the afternoon,
And friends would swear he was still in reach
Though she wore an air of gloom.

Nobody actually spoke to them
So it must have been hard to tell,
Which of the couple was really there
And which fallen under a spell,
The law of shadows is crystal clear
If you're there, a shadow is cast,
The sun shines through if it isn't you
For that's its primary task.

It happens I knew the guy quite well
And he had shadow to spare,
While she was much more ephemeral,
Was somebody not quite there.
I wondered what had attracted him
For she gave out a spray of gloom,
There wasn't that gay affinity
That could gladly light up a room.

I watched as his life force faded away,
His shadow to disappear,
I told him he needed to leave that day
Or the end of his world was near.
But she reached out, and shooed me away,
Seized hold of his wavering hand,
Her eyes burned bright with an evil light,
While his were blank and bland.

I know that we never conversed again
I'd see him afar by day,
She clung on tight to his fading light
As she marched him around the bay,
He hadn't a shadow left to throw
When at last he died on the beach,
Condemned by her to a living hell
As his life slipped out of reach.

He was laid to rest at St. Mary's Cross
While I waited for her to pass,
To see if the shadow she stole from him
Would still cleave to her, at last.
But sunbeams shone through her mourning veil
There was only mine could save,
While I made sure as I stepped one back
That she'd die by my brother's grave.

Poisonous Beauty

The flowers grew from the craters where
The bombs ripped open the ground,
Back in that terrible time of war
When God in his heavens frowned,
I just remember destruction, piles
Of bricks where houses had stood,
And years along, new growth began
Where Airmen lay in the wood.

Their plane came down in the poplar trees
That had stood in a long, straight line,
Tearing a swathe of destruction through
Where we'd played in a former time,
And just beyond was the surgeon's house
That had boasted a Roman Spa,
Now flat, and exposing the Roman Tiles
That survived the previous war.

I'd go down there with Priscilla, who
Lived out by the railway track,
We'd play our games in the cellars
That had lain open, since the attack.
I hadn't taken much notice of
The flowers that grew in the weeds,
That sprang into life like mushrooms, when
The bombs had scattered their seeds.

Priscilla did, she would smell the scent
That had wafted up from the flowers,
And say, 'I've never seen these before,
They're new, they're meant to be ours.'
She'd pick the flowers and take them home
And attempt to make them thrive,
But once removed from their sacred ground
They'd rarely stay alive.

I didn't handle the flowers as much
So I wasn't quite as ill,
When she went down with a jaundice that
The doctors couldn't heal.
They tried their best and they traced it to
The flowers she'd taken home,
A level of radioactivity
Was the reason that they'd grown.

The ground has been cordoned off for good
With a special yellow tape,
While she and I are forbidden to go
To the place that was our escape.
They keep her tied to a wheelchair where
They attempt to hide her sores,
While I'm in a sort of cage since I
Grew skin like the dinosaurs.

The Dragon Ship

I knew she was Scandinavian
With those plaits in her flaxen hair,
And her eyes were such a brilliant blue
They were quite beyond compare,
I'd watch her make her way to the beach
Down the stony clifftop way,
But didn't know she was waiting for him
Till I saw them come that day.

I doubt if she understood our tongue
Though trapped on an English shore,
I'd greet her as I'd greet anyone
With a wave and a smile, for sure,
But she'd bow her head, and hurry away
Determined we shouldn't meet,
I little knew where her secret lay
Though I'd pass her along the street.

She seemed to live in a cottage that
Had been tumbling down for years,
Up on a tuft of poverty grass
That time had dismayed, and cursed,
Her clothes, designed in a northern clime
Must have been hand-sewn with twine,
The colours faded, the patterns run
But to me, she was more than fine.

I watched her all through the Autumn as
She wandered along the beach,
She always stopped at the same old spot
Where the rocks had formed a breach,
The waves would part as they hit the rocks
And a plume sprayed in the air,
Forming a mist of droplets that would
Glisten, all through her hair.

Then winter came in a fury with
Its grey and its fretful skies,
And storms were lashing the seafront
Keeping us home, those who were wise,
But she still ventured abroad some days
Though the wind would take her breath,
And make her stagger along the path
Till I thought she'd catch her death.

Something drove her along that path
For she seemed to be obsessed,
The days were dark, you could barely see,
You'd think that those rocks were blessed,
She'd come back up in an hour or so
With her clothes so soaked and wet,
That once I called, and she came right in,
The first time that we'd met.

She couldn't answer my questions though,
She spoke in a foreign tongue,
One that was heard in northern climes
Back when the world was young,
And when she dried, she walked away
But pointed out to the sea,
And mouthed a single word, a name,
'Brynjar', it had seemed to me.

That night a terrible storm began,
A storm like I'd never seen,
With dense black rolling thunder clouds
That lightning lit, between,
I watched as she wandered out once more
And I looked down to the shore
And noticed a strange old sailing ship
Like I'd seen in a book, before.

The prow was high, and a dragon's head
Stared snarling out through the hail,
A huge square sail was fluttering,
Torn in the raging gale,
And at the prow a warrior, who
Clung onto an oar and spar,
While from the shore, a sudden scream
Had cut through the air, 'Brynjar!'

The ship was swept on the jagged rocks
That had formed a solid breach,
And shattered, as it had broken its back,
To spill its men on the beach,
But Brynjar, lost on the self-same rocks
Caused her to scream, at last,
Just as that scene had faded out
A long lost scene from the past.

I never once saw that girl again,
It's now that I think I know,
How desperate things return sometimes
In a sort of afterglow,
For Brynjar's ship was a Dragon ship
From a thousand years before,
Whose Viking crew came for who knows who,
Trapped on the English shore.

The Icing on the Cake

When Kelvin threatened to cut my throat
I thought him a little stressed,
We'd known each other for twenty years
The first ten were the best,
But I was married to Jill back then
Way back before the divorce,
Then Kelvin lunged, and married her when
Our marriage had run its course.

He seemed to think I was jealous then,
He thought he had hurt my pride,
I thought that our friendship might be saved
Despite his second-hand bride,
'Why would I want her back,' I said,
Hoping to reassure,
But he obsessed and was quite distressed
Each time I came to his door.

'Keep well away from my wife,' he said,
As if I'd not had enough,
'What do you think a divorce is, Kel?
I'm finished with all that stuff.'
'You had your time, you should keep away,
I know that you want her still…'
'As much as I'd want a hole in the head,
You have to believe me, Kel.'

But he just circled the wagons round
Trying to keep her from me,
I'd been quite happy to put her down
Then live my life and be free,
He'd never heard the old saw that said
That to make her yours, let her go,
If she comes back home, then she's yours my friend,
But if not, she wasn't you know.

I saw Jill out in the supermart
And her face was lined and drawn,
I tried to hide by the Brussel Sprouts
But she caught me up by the lawn.
She seemed determined to seek me out,
To see if I looked like hell,
Was disappointed when I looked round
And said I was doing well.

'I'm not,' she said, and a tiny tear
Appeared, to roll down her cheek,
'He never leaves me alone, I fear,
I've been locked in for a week.'
I waved my hand, tried to get away
'Your life is not my concern,'
Then she clung onto my arm and cried,
'I don't know which way to turn!'

And that's when Kelvin himself appeared
And threatened to cut my throat,
It looked as if I had interfered
'And that,' I said, 'is a joke!'
But Jill still clung to my arm beside
The beans, and packets of stew,
'I wish we hadn't divorced,' she said,
'It was so much better with you.'

You'd think a friendship of twenty years
Could overcome such a jest,
But Kelvin suddenly burst in tears
And beat a riff on my chest.
I'll soon get over the broken ribs
And the eye, with a lump of steak,
But Kel's still married to Jill, thank god,
That's the icing on the cake.

The Flowerbed Phone

The phone had only been on a day
When the cranky calls began,
'Nobody knows we're on,' I said,
When at first the damn thing rang.
I had to run up the passageway
To catch it before it stopped,
Then there was just an awesome hush
Like a tree before it's lopped.

The line dropped out at the first 'hello'
As if they would wait for me
To run the length of the passageway,
Expend all that energy,
I'm sure they laughed as they cut me off
Though of course, I couldn't hear,
'It's dead again,' I would rage and froth
'Though it must be someone near.'

'It better not be your stupid friend,'
I said to my wife, Diane,
'The one that's such a comedienne
Who annoys me when she can.'
'It isn't her,' was Diane's reply
In her testy, haughty tone,
'She wouldn't ring when she knows I'm here,
But wait till you're home alone.'

But the phone rang every evening,
At the high point of our show,
Just as they named the villain, and
I nodded to her to go.
'You go,' she'd say, 'I've worked all day,
And it really is your phone,'
I'd grit my teeth up the passageway
And rage at it on my own.

I finally let it ring and ring
And refused to pick it up,
'I'll teach them never to mess with me,'
As I drank a second cup,
A truck arrived in the morning and
It dumped a ton of twine
Blocking all of the driveway while
Some clown said it was mine!

'I never ordered this blasted twine,
You should have come to the door,
Confirmed the order you say you had,
What would I want it for?'
'We got the order over the phone
So we rang, with no reply,
Somebody said you don't pick up
You're such an eccentric guy.'

I always answered it after that,
And after the pig dung treat,
Fifteen tons, and the smell had hung
The length of our angry street,
We tried to tell them it wasn't us
We said it must be the phone,
I know that I would have picked it up
If only I had been home.

We never did get a proper call,
One where somebody spoke,
I don't think anyone likes me, and
That phone's a pig in a poke,
I went outside and I cut the cord
To the world who scorned our line,
Then went inside where the blasted phone
Still rang, one final time.

I picked it up and I snapped, 'Who's that!'
And a voice came on the line,
It wasn't a voice I knew, it spat
And it gruffly asked the time,
'You've cut us off from the Internet,
I hope you're feeling spry,
We live in your rhododendrons, and
You've made the fairies cry!'

The Ten-0-One

We hadn't been in the house for long,
We'd moved in overnight,
I hadn't explored the neighborhood,
As a kid, that wasn't right,
But the only time I had to see
After the daily chores,
Was after dark when my bike and me
Were free to roam outdoors.

I'd had to go to a brand new school
And I met this creepy kid,
He seemed to be breaking every rule
With the cazy things he did,
But I was the only friend he had
So he'd meet me after dark,
And we would ride through the neighborhood
And down through the Chestnut Park.

He said that he'd lived there all his life
Did I really want a thrill?
He'd take and show me where Noah's Ark
Was buried under the hill,
Or maybe I'd like to see the train
That they called the Ten-0-One,
Whose boiler blew in the evening dew
And dismembered everyone.

The night was right for a ghostly tale
There was neither Star nor Moon,
In truth the sky had been overcast
Since the early afternoon,
We rode our bikes to the railway track
On the far side of the park,
I couldn't see either path or tree
As we rode there in the dark.

At almost ten we could hear the train
As it laboured up the hill,
And then the sparks from its stack were seen
In the smoke it chuffed out still,
It loomed up black, and covered in soot
And I looked to see my friend,
Who stood on top of the tender coal
As it passed me on the bend.

I called out, 'How did you get up there?'
As he danced, while looking scared,
A crazy look in his eyes up where
The glow from the fire box flared,
'Come up,' he screamed, 'or you'll miss the fun,'
But the train ran down the hill,
And left me stood by the bike he left
While I felt a sudden chill.

The sky lit up with the brightest light
That I've ever seen, I swear,
But even so, there wasn't a sound
As the train blew up out there,
It left me shivering in the dark
There wasn't a thought of fun,
I'd caught a glimpse of my watch before
It was just on Ten-0-One.

I rode back down the following day
To dispel the fear I felt,
My creepy friend had gone away
Though his bike lay where I knelt,
The railway line from a distant time
Was rusted and lay undone,
For never a train in eighty years
Had followed that Ten-0-One.

Surviving the Flood

The barge slid on through the rushes,
Where once was a major road,
And pushed its way through the bushes
Where the ocean had overflowed,
The draught of the barge was shallow,
We could navigate by the shore,
Or over the swampy marshland to
The remains of the Foodland Store.

'The place is probably empty,'
Said Rob, who sat at the prow,
Hugging the butt of the .22
That we'd need for protection now,
'We'll wait till the stroke of midnight,'
Said Penny, who managed the food,
And nobody thought to argue,
Or put the girl in a mood.

But then, as we rounded the Plaza
Another barge came in view,
'That beast is called 'The Marauder',
Said Rob, who claimed that he knew.
Then lead slammed into our wooden prow
Their method for warning us off,
So Rob fired back with our .22
To show that we weren't so soft.

But that was the end of the stand-off,
They'd loaded their barge and were gone,
Slipping away before ten o'clock
With the tide rising over the lawn.
'We'd better get moving,' our Penny said,
And headed off into the store,
There wasn't much left on the shelves in there,
Some tins, but there wasn't much more.

'I never believed Global Warming,'
Said Rob, as he checked through his list,
'Who would believe that the seas would rise
Or the end of the world be like this?'
'It came on us suddenly,' I replied,
'Too sudden to sandbag the shore,
And everyone fled, unless they were dead,
Up into each mountain and tor.'

'The cities are all under water,
The water is flooding the plain,
We're lucky that Rob found this drifting barge,
It's dirty, but keeping us sane.'
'We're not going to last on the food we have,'
Said Penny, 'we have to find more,'
'We'll chase that 'Marauder', it may come to murder,
But they'd do the same, that's for sure!'

It took us a week to catch their old barge,
They'd run out of fuel, were adrift,
And Rob shot the wretch who'd slept on his watch,
Their barge was half jammed in a ditch.
We transhipped the food while the tide was out,
And left with provisions to spare,
'It's a harsh, cruel world,' we said to their girl,
As we sank their 'Marauder' right there.

Our lives will be fraught as we pass back and forth
On the waters that cover the towns,
We'll have to go diving in Supermarts
For treasures of food that have drowned.
But other survivors are living afloat
Who will try to take over our barge,
The world of the future, a perilous sea,
While there are still others at large.

The Rescue

Madison mounted her coal black mare
In the yard of the Smugglers Inn,
Her coat was black and her hair was fair
And her jodhpurs tucked well in,
The sky was in a threatening mood
With its thunderheads from hell,
As lightning forked on the ancient rood
And the rain teemed down as well.

'You need to get to the Laird,' I cried,
'Tell him to haste to me,
Another day and she may have died,
I'm trying to set her free.
But the Pikemen stand outside her door
And they say they guard her skin,
There were locks and chains on her door before
Up there, in the Smugglers Inn.'

'Tell him to bring his gallant troop
To dismay the Duke of Bray,
He means to imprison his daughter
In his tower, the Lady Grey,'
The Pikemen said that I'd lose my head
If I tried to breach her door,
And wouldn't answer whenever I asked,
'What is she locked in for?'

So Madison wheeled the mare around
And she put it to the spur,
If any could ride a horse to ground
I knew that it was her,
She headed off to the Castle Croft
Head bent to the driving rain,
With lightning flashing around her mount
I watched her across the plain.

What seemed to take forever, I thought,
Was merely an hour or two,
But then my fears were set at naught
As the troop came jangling through.
Each man had raised his sabre and
He'd kept his powder dry,
My heart was surging within me as
The troop came riding by.

And then, at last, was Madison
Still riding with the Laird,
Determined then to save her friend,
To show her that she cared.
The Pikemen soon were beaten down
Were lost in the affray,
I never did catch a glimpse of him,
Their lord, the Duke of Bray.

It took a moment to smash the locks
On the door of Lady Grey,
And all the troop had cheered out loud
As the chains, they fell away.
Madison was the first in line
To embrace the one within,
But we were not to know what lay
Up there, in the Smugglers Inn.

The Lady, held in a firm embrace
Had staggered out through the door,
But blood and pustules were on her face
Like we'd never seen before.
A dying Pikemen called, 'You fools,
You've unleashed a bitter ague,
And then he sighed just before he died,
'Behold, you have the plague!'

The Room in the Albert Mall

The Albert Mall was a narrow street
Named after the dying prince,
Where Queen Victoria donned the rags
Of a widow, ever since.
She'd sat outside in her royal Coach
And been heard to mutter, 'Why?'
While Albert did what he had to do,
What he had to do was die!

And we came by when the Queen was dead
When the Mall was quite forgot,
To rent a room where the prince had died
If we'd known, we'd rather not.
The Mall was grubby and cheap by then
So we thought we'd make it do,
I asked Marie if she didn't mind
And she said, 'It's up to you.'

It seems the room had been empty then
By the choking layers of dust,
I said, 'Shall I let it blow outside?'
And Marie said, 'If you must.'
It took us days just to clear the air
And to have a look around,
In some of the ancient furniture
You can imagine what we found.

The robe held some of the smartest clothes
I think, that we'd ever seen,
I said as much to Marie, 'that dress
You'd swear, was fit for a queen,
And there, a suit for a gentleman
With a full blown grey Top Hat,
I said to Marie, 'Shall we try them on,'
And she said, 'Let's do just that.'

So then on the eve of Michaelmas
We stood by the mirror there,
Arrayed in the best of formal gear
They called Victorian wear,
And music drifted up through the floor
From the ballroom down below,
While I, in a moment of madness
Blurted out, 'Well, shall we go?'

We made our way to the music by
Descending a curving stair,
And finding a throng of dancers who
Were dressed the way we were,
Then someone called out 'Her Majesty,'
And the music stayed and died,
While they all stared at Marie and bowed,
Made me feel queer inside.

I swear that they only saw the clothes,
They didn't see us two,
And they were a shade ephemeral,
I could see right through them, too,
They went right back to their dancing
While we sat on an ottoman,
Whispering what were our chances if
We just got up, and ran.

But then they gradually faded, and
The music died away,
And we were left in an empty room
Before the light of day,
The clothes went back in the dusty robe
And we found another flat,
For just one night we were Prince and Queen
And we're both in awe of that.

Waiting for You!

I wasn't impressed with the spiked black railings
Keeping the residents in,
They swept around to the padlocked gates
Like a prison for mortal sin,
But the signs said 'Happiness Reigns Within –
The end of their lives secure,'
'The Five Star Capital Home for Nursing,
Bring your old to our door.'

I'd only gone to be shown around,
I'd said my aunt wasn't safe,
She wouldn't stay in her cottage grounds
But wandered all over the place.
She needed care, 'which is why I'm here,'
I said, but really I lied,
Some friends had asked I embrace the task
To get a good look inside.

I got to wander around the grounds,
I even shook off the guide,
I settled down in their dim-lit lounge
And watched for the ones that cried.
A woman, clad in a shawl was there,
Who wept, so no-one could see,
Who dabbed her eyes, then in some surprise
She sat there, staring at me.

I didn't think she'd remember me
We were friends some years before,
But she'd succumbed to dementia then
While scrubbing the kitchen floor,
She'd wandered out in a busy street
Was almost hit by a bus,
The ambulance driver said, 'Who's she?'
And I said, 'She's one of us.'

I noticed then, she never came home
And her husband said, 'She's gone!'
He wasn't too stable then himself
And he went, before too long.
I sat with her in the Nursing Home
And I held her trembling hand,
She said she didn't remember me
But she asked me, where was Sam?

The question came as a shock to me
For her husband, Sam, was there,
From where she sat she could surely see
Him straight across, in a chair,
They'd seen each other each day, it seems
He'd not remembered a trace,
Their marriage lost in swirl of dreams
And she'd forgotten his face.

I tried to trigger their memories
Remind them that they had loved,
Had lived together for fifty years
Whenever he'd pushed, she shoved.
But Jennifer took one look at Sam
And twisted her gaze away,
'I'm certain he couldn't be my man,
He has so little to say.'

When next I heard, she had gone back home,
Her mind as clear as a bell,
My friends said I must have shaken her up,
They'd never seen her so well.
But still she wept for her Sam at night,
Said where on earth could he be,
So I went back to that house of hell,
Brought Sam back out on a 'Free'.

Some places hold their own loving spell,
The very air is bewitched,
And Jennifer's house was enchanted with
A spell from the house to the ditch.
When she saw Sam on the bluebell path
Uncertain of what to do,
She rushed straight into his arms and cried,
'My love, I've been waiting for you!'

Black Goth

'Why do you colour your lips so black,
Darken your piercing eyes,
What are you hiding behind your back,
Have you been telling me lies?
Why are you wearing those knee length boots,
Pulling that cloak round, tight,
Where are you going, under the Moon,
Where will you be tonight?

Christabel grimaced but wouldn't reply,
She turned, with her hand on the door,
Gazing right through me, I'd thought that she knew me
But there was no love like before.
Her brows, they were furrowed, her eyes hard as glass,
Her lips they were pursed in contempt,
I should have left then when she'd put down the pen
But I didn't know then what it meant.

I knew she was moody, I knew she was dark,
She'd flutter round blind, like a moth,
She always wore black, even out in the park,
They warned me, they said 'She's a Goth!'
I'd found her entrancing at first, I admit,
I tried to get into her mind,
But once in those raveling tunnels of darkness
The deepest of thoughts were unkind.

I picked up the note she left screwed on the floor
The moment she left for the night,
'I have to see Jack,' she had scribbled, 'That's that!'
I must put my nightmares to flight.'
I knew there was darkness and heartache to come,
She'd promised him plenty of strife,
But then I'd jumped in to his bucket of sin
As I thought she was out of his life.

I asked her at first was she over him yet,
And yes, she assured me she was,
But surely his name wouldn't drive her insane
If it wasn't a question of loss!
A terrible feeling came over me then,
I needed to know where she went,
So headed on out to where Jack hung about,
I shouldn't have gone, I repent.

I saw through the window the angel of death
Her cloak streaming out, like a moth,
And he in the corner, not catching his breath
His throat in the grip of a Goth!
I tried to burst in but the door was deadlocked,
I saw the knife raised in her fist,
Then plunge, and a scream like some terrible dream,
For just as he died, she had kissed!

She came out toward me but covered in blood,
On hands, on her lips and her face,
While I backed away, I had nothing to say,
But, 'Heaven above, lend me grace!'
She ran away, stumbling, on through the dark
But she'd not seen her nightmares off,
I found she was hung on a light in the park,
In her mouth was a fluttering moth.

Halloween

Somebody said it was Halloween
I hadn't a clue till then,
But the street was full of pumpkin heads
Carved out, with the candles in,
And the kids kept saying 'trick or treat'
Though I didn't know what for,
They must have thought I was pretty dumb
As I shooed them away from my door.

Then Mandy came out dressed as a witch
With a cloak and a pointy hat,
And waving a broom they call a 'swish',
'So what is the point of that?'
'Tonight the witches fly to their mass,
Under a harvest moon,
Shut your eyes as the broomsticks pass
Or they'll put you to sleep, till noon.'

I thought I'd better prepare myself
So broke out my scatter gun,
The moment a witch would show herself
I swore that I'd have some fun,
With Jack O' Lanterns the only light
As the night grew evil and dark,
I almost forgot that we lived next door
To the Mountainous Ski-Lift Park.

There wasn't a Moon that eerie night,
It must have been hid by a cloud,
I could hear the chatter of witches, laughing,
How could they be so loud?
At midnight all of the chatter stopped
And everything went so still,
Just as the Moon popped out of the cloud
And the witches flew over the hill.

I saw their shapes up against the sky
Riding their broomsticks there,
With warty noses and pointy hats
And horrible tangled hair,
I didn't think, I just raised my gun
And I blasted a spray of shot,
And watched each witch as she fell to earth
Whether they would, or not.

Mandy screamed and she seized the gun,
Ripped it out of my hands,
'Have you gone crazy, what have you done?'
She wouldn't cease her demands.
'I saw them flying, up on their brooms,
I blew them out of the air.'
'They didn't fly, they just held on tight
Under the Ski-Lift chair.'

Whenever Halloween comes around
I tend to stay in my room,
And woe betide any witch that tries
Approaching me with a broom,
While Mandy locks up my scatter gun,
(That's the one thing that will chafe),
Then goes to the witches at the door,
'Yes, the Ski-Lift chair is safe!'

The House in the Lane

There's not much of anything I can recall
From the time that we lived in the lane,
Only the puddles of rainwater eddying
With the wind's gusting refrain.
Pamela knew, she was older than me
So absorbed all the essence of fear,
And many a time when she'd panic and whine
I would cry out 'There's nobody here!'

The trees were too tall and they ruled overall
By keeping the house in their shade,
The garden was cold and the rocks would grow mould
From the damp, in the part that I played.
The wind would come sniffing around from the trees
And shiver the hairs on my spine,
And then in a wheeze like a voice in the breeze,
'You shouldn't be here, this is mine!'

Our parents were never around it would seem,
Our time was spent mostly alone,
It's true that I grew to be sensitive, too,
To the visions and sounds of my own.
But Pamela, she became crazy with fear
At every strange creak in that house,
So then when she'd scream, I'd say, 'It's a dream,'
And place a cloth over her mouth.

The house was three storeys, we never went up
To check out the topmost floor,
They said it was storage, and not ours to forage
So kept a stout lock on the door,
But Pamela said she heard noises above,
Like somebody padding around,
It couldn't have been, or they would have been seen
Between the third floor and the ground.

But out from the garden I'd often look up
To stare at the sole window pane,
The one that was muddy, or could it be bloody,
The colour was almost the same.
It was strange they insisted the stairway was locked
Could there be a grim secret to hide,
The darkest of murders, hidden away
And the storeroom above? Well, they lied!

Then Pamela said that she saw someone,
A shadow that fell on the pane,
Strange that the mud had continued in place
In spite of the seasonal rain.
Muddy or bloody, it wouldn't wash off
Though I stared and I stared, and I smiled,
The indistinct face that I saw staring back
Was the face of an evil child.

They say that the rest was over to me
Though I'll never recall if it's true,
It's funny the things that you do in life
That you never thought you could do.
Pamela said I was quite the brat
But then Pamela's such a liar,
All I recall is the face of a child
As the flames in the window grew higher.

A Question of Faith

'I'd swear that the sun is hotter,' she said,
'It's hotter than I can recall,
The garden's turned into a desert, is dead
My plants are fried up to the wall.'
I said I agreed, the car was so hot
I often got scorched by the steel,
The belt with the buckle was always red hot
And so was the steering wheel.

I said you could tell by the state of the road
Could tell by the bitumen melt,
The surface was shiny with liquefied tar
The heat off the surface you felt.
Beyond was the countryside, brown and bereft
Not a single green shoot could you see,
The bushes were brown from the top to the ground
And there wasn't a leaf on a tree.

'The place is like tinder, it just needs a spark
And it all will go up with a roar,'
We couldn't survive in the smoke from the park,
We would have to be gone, well before.
I told Desdemona to pack us a case,
Just those things we would need on the run,
Some food and some water, a doll for our daughter,
Remember to pack us a gun.

We took it in turns to keep watch through the night,
To listen to every slight breeze,
The heat was intense, we looked over the fence
For any strange light through the trees,
It came from the valley, that terrible roar
So we knew that the demon was out,
Some one lit a spark way down in the park
And Des raised the house with a shout.

The three of us piled in the four wheel drive
And headed up over the hill,
The terror of flames in the rear view mirror
Have plagued and have haunted me still.
The wind had been gusting and fanning the flames
Pursuing us on our retreat,
Had crept up beside us and threatened to ride
Ahead to our certain defeat.

The heat so intense it had cracked the screen
And blistered the paint on the door,
When Desdemona let out a scream
To point to the gun on the floor.
'Is this why you asked me to pack the gun,
Is it either that, or burn?'
I'd not meet her eyes with a tissue of lies
So I masked my own concern.

I heard her pray as the tyres caught fire
And exploded, one by one,
I kept the pedal flat to the floor,
It was either that, or the gun.
Then out of the darkness loomed a lake,
It was water up to the doors,
We came to rest where the water blessed
With the fire held back by the shores.

The skies were grey and they opened up
With God's good grace at the dawn,
I held my wife and my daughter close
As the rain made us feel reborn,
When the people tell me there is no God
I just smile, and I let them go,
If he isn't there then I find it odd
That he sent the rain... I know!

The Abbot's Loft

They bet me I couldn't spend the night
Locked up in the Abbot's loft,
Up where recusants once, in fright
Would wait for the stake at Pentecost.
They'd once piled faggots high in the square
And taunted all night long,
When peasants stood in the firelight
In a massive, cheering throng.

But that was hundreds of years ago
So of course I said I could,
I should have known there was something wrong
When I saw the man in the hood,
The loft was next to the church bell tower
And would creak when they pulled the rope
Of the giant bell that sat in its bower
To wait commands from the Pope.

I climbed the circular, rickety stair
And they came and locked me in,
There wasn't a spark of light in there
It was dark, as black as sin,
And all there was was a narrow bed
On a hard, old wooden plank,
A single cover to keep me warm
But I knew just who to thank.

They played the silliest games, of course,
They would howl outside the door,
Just as I started to settle down
I would hear this terrible roar,
Somehow the timbers would start to creak
When they put a strain on the rope,
And then the bell with a sound like hell
Would boom, and I'd almost choke.

I lay the night in a fevered sleep
But I swear someone came in,
I felt a breeze from the open door
And that coarse, harsh breath of sin,
But then a gurgling, choking sound
As my hair stood up on end,
I stayed curled up in my dark surround
As the door creaked once, then slammed.

When morning came, a sliver of light
Shone in through a rafter beam,
It fell upon a terrible sight
A nightmare, wrapped in a dream,
A man, whose body lay by the bed
His throat all ragged and torn,
And blood in puddles of horrible dread,
I wished I'd never been born.

They must have rushed on up to my screams
Flung open the padlocked door,
Then stood in silence, staring at me
And what lay dead on the floor,
I saw him then, the man in the hood
He'd wanted someone to blame,
And there I was, all covered in blood
With friends to witness my shame.

They'd bet me I couldn't spend the night
Locked up in the Abbot's loft,
Up where recusants once, in fright
Would wait for the stake at Pentecost.
But now my nights are spent in a cell
Dreaming of death and blood,
And why he'd want to send me to hell
That infamous man in the hood.

The Poetry Barn

The Poetry Barn wasn't really a barn
It was merely an old farm house,
It sat on the acres of Eddington's Farm,
Surrounded by sheep and by cows.
But Poets came over from Stuttersby Dell,
Drove over from Scatabout Wood,
To write in the air of the Poetry Barn
About things, when they ought and they should.

They came from Great Orton, they came from Rams Well,
They came from Glenn Forage and Grey,
The best and the worst of the poets you'd find
At the Poetry Barn, every day,
The rooms had been empty for many a year
So they all sat on bundles of straw,
And when they ran out they would send up a shout,
So some would go out and get more.

The mornings would see all the Elegies worked,
The Epics, the Odes and Quatrains,
The Poetry Barn would then grumble and groan
As the Dirges would enter the drains.
By noon the fair Sonnets came into their own
With just the odd wanton Lament,
When poets would seek out the culprit to find
One grinding his verse in a tent.

145

By evening they'd work on the Pastoral,
The Sestet, the Roundel as well,
And those at a loss after losing the toss
Would be stuck with the old Villanelle,
They'd all settle down when the Moon came up round,
And the stars twinkled boldly in rhyme,
When one asked the other, 'pray, what rhymes with brother,'
And he'd say, 'your Mom, all the time.'

The poems would stick to the inside walls,
Would tear at each other like knaves,
They'd fill up the aisles and lie flat on the tiles
And would damage the old architraves.
At night you could hear all the horses hooves
As they carried the good news to Aix,
And in came the wedding guest, him with the albatross
Counting his many mistakes.

I saw that they'd burned down the Poetry Barn
With one sad, incendiary rhyme,
A poet called Glover who wrote to his lover
'My candle, you light all the time.'
The straw caught alight in his lover's delight
And they fled from that bastion of verse,
I just penned this missal for someone to whistle,
The one that he'd written was worse.

Into the Light

When I was a great deal younger than today, and first embarked on poetry, I made a decision to write a one verse poem every ten years, starting at the age of 21. This was to reflect the way I felt at the time, in relation to my life, and to my writing. The following is the verse offered for the age of seventy-one, and below that the complete verses that built up to this point. The collection is called... Into the Light.

VI

Here I am, seventy-one
They say that only the good die young,
I've made the most of my current plight
To find dark corners, to sit and write,
The Chinese taught me their own folk lore
And Poe his raven, above the door,
So now I've written a thousand tales
Of shifting time and of dragon's scales
While things I thought that would bring undone
Before the age of seventy-one
Have left me sat in my garret webs
To pen the last, to the final dregs,
I know where to head, the time is right,
    Out of the darkness
      Into the light!

I

Here I am, twenty-one,
So many things have to be done,
Many's the cause I'll be fighting for
Keeping the vows that I've sworn before,
How many children blessing my way,
How much love can a lover sway,
How many words can I write and read
In the years ahead for my restless need,
Where am I headed, this fateful night…
Out of the darkness
Into the light!

II

Here I am, thirty-one,
So many things still to be done;
Where are the causes? Fought and lost!
What of the vows? Tempest tossed!
Where are the children? Left behind!
What of the lovers? Love is blind!
How many words have you written and read?
Much too much for this aching head.
Where are you headed, this fateful night?
Out of the darkness
Into the light!

III

Here I am, forty-one,
And all life seems like a dream undone.
Everything I would have taken for me
Has slipped from my grasp, forsaken me.
All my children are grown, but one
And wonder; 'Where did this man come from?
What was the pact that he kept with me…'
While I have nothing to answer thee.
All my words as a mist, widespread
Have since dispersed from a source long dead.
Where am I headed, this fateful night?
  (Have you learned nothing….?)
   I guess you're right!

IV

Here I am, fifty-one,
The daylight fades and the muse has gone.
The loves I loved as my vision bled
All turned from me, and to them, I'm dead.
The rhyme was lost and the music died
As I turned to stone in my heart, inside.
Where is the youth that yearned to write
Through the endless days to the latest night?
Is this what happens, the years take flight –
  Into the darkness
   Out of the light.

V

Here I am, sixty-one,
I thought the end would have come and gone!
But then a light seemed to beckon me
To trip through another's history.
When China called, I know not why
I saw new future's I'd never tried,
The way was clear, my life was spent
So I fetched up in the Orient.
With all its bustle, its pomp, and pride,
I picked up the pen that I'd put aside,
For black-haired girls feed my heart's content
And children like jewels are heaven sent;
Is this the future, I know it's right....
        Out of the darkness
        Into the light!

Crossing the Bridge

I was out when the heavens opened up,
I was only but halfway there,
I hadn't a coat or umbrella then
On my way to my darling dear,
But she was dry in her great big house
That was built up high on the ridge,
The river rose and it blocked my path
With the Warlock, guarding the bridge.

His hat was wet and his cloak had flared
While his eyes, pinpoints of red,
Stood out from under his hat and stared
As my mind was filled with dread,
I didn't know if he'd let me pass
I had met his type before,
He was grumble-growl with a werewolf's howl
And a sharp and mighty claw.

I tried to pass on the narrow bridge
But he growled, 'Who goes you where?'
I said, 'I'm going to meet my girl
In the house on the ridge up there.'
'You shall not pass, you shall not go,
I shall tear you limb from limb,'
His claws he raised in a grisly show
And his jaw was set and grim.

The rain continued its pelting down
And the thunder pealed above,
I felt determined to beat this clown
I was fortified with love.
'You'll not be wanting to cross Nyrene
She will drop a spell or two,
That will tear apart your Warlock's heart
When her spell is done with you.'

The Warlock started to make reply
When the lightning hit the rail,
And lit him up like a paper cup
From his head down to his tail,
The river washed him across the bridge
And into its raging flow,
Whether he drowned or fried that day
Well really, I wouldn't know.

'You shouldn't have used my name in vain,'
Nyrene told me at the door,
'That lightning flash may have caused you pain,
It was kept in my 'Un-aimed' Store.'
I never go up if the rivers rise
When Nyrene's home on the ridge,
If lightning's lurking up in the skies
Or a Warlock's guarding the bridge.

The Share

The flats were old and the rooms were cold
But I didn't have much choice,
I hadn't the money for anything else
Since the spat I had with Joyce,
I'd walked the streets for almost a day
Just to find a place to stay,
When I finally found a flat to rent
The building was old and grey.

Dust was grimed on the windowsill
And mud was tramped in the hall,
Whatever was left of the carpet there
You just couldn't see at all,
The caretaker in the bottom flat
Handed out the do's and don'ts,
The rent on time on the topmost line,
Ahead of the wills and won'ts.

I didn't know it was partly share
Till I'd paid, and taken the key,
Until I entered the bathroom there
And found there was more than me.
A woman sat there, painting her nails
Come in from the flat next door,
Said, 'You're my share?' as she patted her hair,
'You'd better prepare, there's more.'

We not only shared the bathroom there
But the key to the only Loo,
There was only a single kitchen there
And it looked like we shared that too,
I wasn't impressed, was more than depressed
And I kept on thinking of Joyce,
How could I sink so low, I thought,
But she didn't give me a choice.

I lay in bed the following morn,
Lay in till a quarter-past two,
Why should I get up early when
There was nothing I had to do.
I thought I'd cook me a rasher or two,
Some eggs, and a slice of bread,
Till I walked out into the kitchen, then
And into a land of dread.

There were bats hung over the fireplace,
And a great big pot on the hob,
And something thin that had just been skinned
Lay over an iron knob.
There were piles of bones on the platter board
And some fingers left on a plate,
Their rings were on but the hand was gone,
Off to a dismal fate.

I whirled about in despair, in case
Someone was stalking me,
And checked the grate of the fireplace
Where the ashes glowed redly,
The pot was bubbling on the hob
And some things that looked like ears,
Kept bobbing up to the surface
Like some headless bombardiers.

I spun away to the kitchen sink
And I gazed into its depths,
Peered on in with a single blink
And I fought to keep my breath,
For staring up was a grinning skull
As the girl I saw last night,
Came leaping in like a beast of sin
And I lost my appetite.

'It isn't what you might think,' she said,
'I should have warned you, right!
We use this room for the local Rep
To rehearse their play tonight.
I set it up for the witches scene,
It's only a plastic skull,
And plastic bats and toy skinned-cats,
Want to eat?' I said 'I'm full!'

The Monster & the Candle

I'd swear a monster lived in the hall
Of the house when I was young,
Just like the tiger under the bed
I could see when they were gone,
For I could hear him climbing the stair
When the house was fast asleep,
I knew he roamed around and about
When the stairs began to creak.

And then he'd enter my bedroom and
He'd re-arrange my toys,
That's how I knew he disliked me, he
Kept all his tricks for boys.
He never bothered my sister, or
Disturbed her dolls and things,
Her bedroom was like a sanctuary
For her necklaces and rings.

He'd hide in all of the daylight hours
So he'd not be seen by them,
The others, who would make fun of me
When I warned them all again:
'You wait, he's going to take you out
He will catch you unawares,
You won't be able to scream or shout
When he comes, and climbs the stairs.'

The winter months were both damp and cold
And the woodwork creaked and groaned,
It shrunk and stretched, it was getting old
And it hid the monster's moans.
So I hid down by the bannister
And I tied a string across,
To trip him when he would climb the stairs,
I would teach the monster loss!

A storm was raging outside that night
And the wind howled through the trees,
The back door opened and flapped a lot
And let in a winter breeze,
I heard my father run down the stairs
And an awful cry and crash,
Then silence settled and fed my fears
Where the bannister was smashed.

I thought the monster was gone for good
With the service come and gone,
I thought he couldn't survive that crash
And the crematorium,
But barely a week had passed us by
And the stairs began to creak,
So I placed a candle under the stair
And the place burned for a week.

The Conquistador

When once we dived on the San Miguel
Off the coast of old Peru,
We little knew that under the swell
Was an Aztec treasure, too.
I scuba'd down, and the vessel lay
Tipped onto its starboard side,
And mostly covered in silt that day
That buried its Spanish pride.

The wreck had never been seen before
So my heart began to pound,
We'd found the ship we'd been looking for
Submerged, and under a mound,
While whisking some of the silt away
My eyes had caught a gleam,
The helmet of a Conquistador
Lay trapped, and under a beam.

But as the silt was dispersed I saw
That the helmet still was full,
For glaring out from beneath its brim
Was a fearsome human skull,
The skeleton was intact, and lay
Still trapped, where once he fell,
His legs were caught in a cannon bay
Of the fated San Miguel.

I had no time for the niceties
That I should have shown to him,
But seized the helmet from off his head
And I left him, looking grim,
I took it up to the surface as
The first of our spoils that day,
And told the crew that I claimed it,
It was mine, so come what may!

The treasure trove was incredible
Of jewels and gold moidores,
I didn't think that my helmet would
Be missed, once taken ashore,
But in my mind was a picture that
I'd seen on the ocean bed,
Of that struggling, drowned Conquistador
And that helmet on his head.

I sat that helmet in pride of place
As a conversation piece,
Tricked it up with a piece of lace
Thanks to a helpful niece,
But then the sounds had begun at night
The clashing of steel on steel,
And shadows, moving in passageways
From something that wasn't real.

One night, the door with a mighty crash
Fell into the passageway,
I must have been feeling more than rash
To venture toward the fray,
For standing there in the open door
Was a skeleton, with a sword,
Who slipped the helmet onto its head
Not saying a single word.

I watched it wade back into the sea
This pile of ancient bones,
And think I know where it's sure to be
Back where it lay, alone,
It seeks its brother Conquistadors
Where each had perished as well,
Guarding the store of gold moidores
In the hold of the San Miguel.

Guardians of the Chest

My father married a scheming witch
The month that my mother died,
He barely waited her final twitch
And it killed something inside,
I suddenly found myself alone
Apart from my brother, Liam,
But my heart inside had turned to stone
And the house was a mausoleum.

I'd hear her wandering round the house
When my father was away,
And something about the air in there
Made me feel some blank dismay,
For Liam was little help to me
He fell to the witch's charm,
I tried to warn, but he looked in scorn
While I only felt alarm.

My father became a wealthy man
When my mother left him all,
She'd been the heir to a ladyship
And the deeds to Woolhampton Hall,
A wooden chest with the whole bequest
Was locked in a basement room,
And giant rocks in a jewel box
Would flash, they said, in the gloom.

But Lara never could find the key
Though she searched, both high and low,
My father never let on he knew
For he'd promised my mother so,
When she had said, with her final breath
'I know all about the witch,
Don't let her near my jewel box
Or you'll end in a pauper's ditch.'

He carried the key most everywhere
In his waistcoat, or his cuff,
He fastened it to his horse's hair
And once to my choirboy's ruff,
So Lara stormed while he was away,
I could hear her scream and curse,
And beat her feet on the basement door,
I didn't know which was worse.

She asked Liam if he'd help her find
The key, and she'd see him right,
I heard him lurking about the house
To our father's room, at night.
I asked him, 'Where is your loyalty,
To your father or the witch?'
But he cursed and said flamboyantly,
'Well, the witch will make me rich!'

'I wouldn't go in that basement room,'
I said, in a word of warning,
Remembering something my mother said
To her mirror, one dark morning,
'I've made it plain in my will,' she said,
'And it's there in the many riders,
Whoever thinks they can steal from me,
Must deal with a world of spiders.'

And so it passed, when Liam at last,
Found out where the key was hiding,
Was taking her to the basement stair
While my father was out, and riding,
I heard the screams in the basement room,
That sounded much like a riot,
By the time that I went to lock them in,
Both he and the witch were quiet!

Slither and Scale

They often walked in the garden, though
The garden was such a mess,
It was overgrown with Ivy, and
Choked up with watercress,
The pond was overflowing its banks
At the wet time of the year,
But no-one tended the garden then
It was much too hard to clear.

The house was old and the walls were damp
It had been a fine estate,
Built up from scratch by the pioneers
Then left to my schoolboy mate,
And now he was nearing twenty-five
And he had Germaine in tow,
I'd thought I could win her heart from him
But I had no place to go.

We lived, we three, in the house where we
Could each survive on our own,
While keeping the others company
Though not quite living alone,
So Paul lived up on the West Wing floor,
Germaine set up in the East,
While I had a couple of rooms downstairs,
In truth, I counted the least.

I stayed away from the garden when
I saw a snake in the pond,
More of a giant serpent that was
Six foot long, and beyond,
I didn't caution the other two
For some strange quirk of my own,
For Paul would walk on the pondward side
While she would wander alone.

I heard her scream as the serpent came
Slithering up from the pool,
My blood ran cold as it struck at Paul,
He was much too close, the fool.
It bit, he said, on the hand and leg
It struck so fast, and had flown,
Then he called out in a chilling shout,
'Its fangs went through to the bone!'

We carried him up in a faint that day
The venom was coursing his veins,
I must admit I was glad of it
For I only thought of Germaine.
She saw me stare at her auburn hair
And she must have known, before,
I'd been so very obsessed with her
But she only thought of Paul.

He lay in a fever there for days,
I thought that he might just die,
But felt ashamed of the thoughts that came,
My friendship caught in a lie,
If only she could have come to me
I could truly call him friend,
But she was true, and it seemed I knew
She would nurse him to the end.

One day she came, he was not the same,
She said, in a tortured tone,
'His skin is starting to scale,' she said,
'He wants to be left alone.
His eyes have turned into tiny slits
And he seems to slither in bed,
His fangs are longer and sharper now
Than ever I've seen,' she said.

I had to go, to see for myself,
I noticed his skin was grey,
His eyes were shifty, flickered about,
I didn't know what to say,
He licked his lips but his tongue was forked
As if he'd split it in two,
His lips drew back and his fangs slid out,
'What do I want with you?'

'I've never seen such a change,' I said,
'How much of what's left is Paul?'
He reared up in the bed at that
And flattened against the wall,
I felt that he was about to strike
So I left the room in a rush,
And told Germaine, 'We had better leave,
Or it might mean the end of us.'

She stuck with Paul to the very end
I think that I knew she would,
They found her lying beside the pond
With her face suffused with blood.
Her skin looked just like a dragon's scales
Her eyes pinpoints, if at all,
They killed two snakes in the garden pond,
There was nobody there called Paul.

The Blank and Future Book

I'd always thought that books were the same,
There wasn't a lot to choose,
They each seep slowly into your brain
With knowledge you can't refuse,
But then a book I found on a shelf
All dirty and dark and dank,
I'd read so far, then turning the page
I'd find every page was blank.

The print will stay till I drop my eyes
And the book slips from my grasp,
Then every page that's ahead is blank
As the book escapes my clasp.
The villain smirks as I lose the plot
And he changes what's to be,
He struggles up from the printed page
In an effort to be free.

I read the book on a cliff top verge
Looking down along the coast,
The day was calm like a soothing balm
And I felt as warm as toast,
My eyelids, heavy as lead dropped down
Preparatory to sleep,
When someone scaling the cliff ahead
Called out, began to weep.

'God help me, sir, or I'll fall below,
On that pile of jagged rocks,
Reach out for me and don't let me go,
You don't look the type that mocks.'
I noticed then that I'd dropped the book
In a pool of mud, and rank,
It fell agape with a broken back
The following pages blank.

'I have to ask how your tale will end,
It's unfinished in the book,
Your villainous deeds go on, and then
Disappear each time I look.'
'It ends any way you want it to,
It's the tale without an end,
For you are the villain in the book
You can do what you intend.'

I stood up straight and I kicked on out
At the figure on the cliff,
And he fell back with a scream, a shout
To the rocks along the reef,
I turned to pick up the broken book
Wiped the pages free from mud,
There wasn't a single page left blank
Each page was stained with blood.

The Second-Hand Gown

He wandered along old Codshill Street,
Quite late on that Christmas Eve,
And scanned the used haberdashery
Society ladies would leave,
The hats they'd worn, but only the once,
The boots with barely a scuff,
The poplin prints they hadn't worn since,
A single dance was enough.

He stood outside in his working boots
The ones he wore at the mill,
He hadn't had time to change himself
He should have been working still.
But in his pocket he clutched the pound
He'd saved for many a day,
He'd squirrelled each shilling away for months
Out of his meagre pay.

And all he could see was Mirabelle,
Who lodged at his heart and eye,
She worked upstairs in the counting room
Above where the shuttles fly,
And he would glimpse her once in a while
Pottering to and fro,
Dressed in a worn and paltry frock
Where the stitching was letting go.

He'd wait outside, and follow her home
To see she was safe and sound,
The rogues that he'd meet in Codshill Street
Would keep their eyes on the ground.
While she was aware of his loving gaze
And sometimes gave him a smile,
Others were bold in their loving ways
And pressed their court for a while.

And so it was on this Christmas Eve
That a Squire had stood at her door,
With a string of pearls you wouldn't believe
He'd bought in a jeweller's store,
And she was flushed as she let him in,
So pleased to have such a gift,
For she was only a working girl
And his interest gave her a lift.

But there in the haberdashery
In a window, stood at the side,
Was standing a model, dressed entire
In a gown so fine, he'd cried.
He thought he could see his Mirabelle
In place of the mannequin,
In the gown of grey crushed velvet, so
In a moment then, went in.

'You know that the gown is second-hand,'
The girl explained to his stare,
'Here are a couple of tiny stains,
And there is a little tear.
But this, that once cost a hundred pounds
Is a bargain now for a cause,
If you can give me a single pound
This lovely gown can be yours.'

She placed the gown in a long flat box,
And tied a ribbon around,
Then he flew out to his Mirabelle
In hopes she still could be found.
He saw the pearls were around her neck
When she had opened the door,
But once she pulled out the gown, she checked,
And dropped the pearls on the floor.

Her kiss was sweet on that Christmas Eve,
Though he had showed her the stains,
The tears she shed on that gorgeous thread
He said, were like summer rains,
She had no time for the wealthy Squire,
She'd waited for him all along,
Her greatest gift was a second-hand gown
With the love that the gown came from.

Turn of the Knife

The sun sat up on the mountain top
And started to sink from view,
A shadow, spread on the valley floor
Was creeping over you,
You'd just told me that you'd had enough
In the shade of a chestnut tree,
And then I saw in your shrouded smile
That you meant you were through with me.

I didn't know what I'd done to you,
I thought it was only love,
But then the shadow had covered you
From the mountain top above,
You pulled your hood up over your hair
And wrapped yourself in your cloak,
Said you were going to leave me there
Go off with some other folk.

Your words were cruel, and pierced my heart
I wasn't aware I'd erred,
You acted as if we'd strayed apart,
There was someone you preferred,
We'd been together so long I thought
That no-one could take my place,
But since you've shown that I'm on my own
I'm afraid of losing face.

And so I lie in the Mulberry bush
And I wait to see him here,
His first embrace with the one I love
Will become his last, I fear,
I took the knife from the kitchen drawer
With a view to bring his end,
But now I see as he ventures near
That the cheating one's my friend.

How could you take my friend from me
As you take yourself away,
It isn't enough that I'm losing you
But my friend as well, today,
I'll not be spilling his blood tonight
As I thought I'd surely do,
But all the anger and hurt I feel
Has turned the knife on you.

Shadows in the Rain

My father told us the story of
The time of his greatest pain,
Back in the year of ninety-nine,
During Victoria's reign,
He lived in a two-bed terrace,
With a brother and sisters two,
With gas lamps out in the cobbled street
And nothing you'd call a view.

'The windows were of a pebble glass
That distorted all you'd see,
And when it rained and the clouds were grained
All these shades appeared to me,
The lamps would cast a flickering beam
On the movement in the street,
To paint in shadows the local scene
Of that place they called 'The Fleet'.'

'I thought these shadows were passing ghosts
Who had died and lost their way,
Their shadows, caught in the pouring rain
Coming back and forth all day,
I little knew that my brother too
Would be claimed before too long,
Would add his tiny, flickering soul
To the heart of that heaving throng.'

'For down below, a river would flow
Underneath the Coach and Horse,
The mighty sewers of the Fleet
Followed that watercourse,
The entrances were underground
And the water in it foul,
But floating bodies were often found
And the sewer men would howl.'

'And Toby, our little Toby, he
Would be sent along the street,
He'd clatter along the cobblestones
For a loaf of bread, a treat,
He'd fetch a plug of tobacco for
Our father's pipe, of course,
Collecting it from the barman there,
Down at the Coach and Horse.'

'He'd toddle away, in light or dark,
He'd go in the sun or rain,
Whatever my father asked him do
He saw no need to explain,
And Toby went in the drizzling rain
One day, for a quart of beer,
I watched for him through the pebble glass
But the lad quite disappeared.'

'All I could see were the moving shapes
Of the shadows in the rain,
Of ghosts, all huddled in coats and capes
As they passed my way, again,
But never a sight of our Toby, nor
The quart of my father's beer,
We sent out a searching party, but
He wasn't to reappear.'

'We got in touch with the sewer men
Who said they would search the Fleet,
And try to find him before he flowed
To the Thames on New Bridge Street,
But all they found were a dozen dogs
Along with a monster pig,
Who all had drowned before they were found
And Toby was half as big.'

'My father stood at the open door
At the same time every day,
Come rain or shine, he couldn't divine
Why Toby had gone away,
But I can see, as if in a fit,
A thing that should count the least,
My father's pipe, forever unlit,
Still gracing the mantelpiece.'

Keeper of the Light

I pulled at the oars with Valentine
While Derek sat at the rear,
He'd taken his turn, now I took mine
Our quarry was drawing near,
For up on the bluff, deserted now
The tower stood, gaunt and white,
We'd managed the creaking boat somehow
To get to the Keystone Light.

It hadn't been manned for fifty years
Its age was a matter of doubt,
The Keeper's wife, in a fit of tears,
Left the light sputtering out.
Her husband gone in a giant wave
That carried him off from the bluff,
While in the dark was the Barque 'Enclave'
Settling down in a trough.

And on the steps of the Keystone Light
The widow clung to the rail,
The wave was tugging about her skirt
As the Barque lost its mizzen sail,
A shark, caught up in the mighty swell
Was swept right up to the steps,
And took her leg in a single bite,
Returned with it to the depths.

178

They found her dead by the Keystone Light
The Barque, smashed up on the shore,
But never a sign of the Keeper, Sam,
Who had guarded the Light before.
They said his ghost ruled the tower top
That it howled in a winter storm,
While she kept swinging the outer door
To try keep the tower warm.

So we climbed up on that winter's day,
The three of us to the bluff,
We lads let Valentine lead the way
She liked all that ghostly stuff.
The door hung off from its hinges there
From flapping about in the wind,
While Derek muttered, 'We'd best beware,
There may be ghosts,' and he grinned.

We'd gone, expecting to stay the night
So carried our candles and gear,
The bottom floor with the open door
Was a little too breezy, I fear.
I followed Valentine up to the Light
And carried the blankets there,
The view was truly a marvellous sight
But the wind gave us all a scare.

It hummed and soughed at the outer rail,
It groaned, and whispered and growled,
They'd warned, 'It sounds like the Keeper's wail,'
And true, at times it had howled.
It even seemed to have called her name,
The widow, crying in pain,
'Caroline, I'll be coming for you,'
Was the sound of the wind's refrain.

We slept that night, or we tried to sleep
All huddled up on the floor,
But Derek rose, and before the dawn
His body lay down on the shore.
He must have fallen over the rail
While both of us were asleep,
But now the sound of the wind in its wail
Said, 'Catch the wave at its peak!'

We hurried on down the spiral stair,
As the dawn came up like a trick,
We couldn't bear to be caught up there
With both of us feeling sick.
But Valentine went out on the steps
Where the widow had stood before.
A sudden gust caught the door and just
Knocked Valentine to the floor.

I saw she'd never get up again
With the wound it gave to her head,
So much blood, like Caroline,
I knew she had to be dead.
I heave away at the oars, and pray
That their sacrifices will be
Enough to bring back my Caroline
For the Lighthouse Keeper was me!

Index of First Lines

183

www.ingramcontent.com/pod-product-compliance
Lightning Source LLC
LaVergne TN
LVHW051632080426
835511LV00016B/2316